ALL VOWS
New and Selected Poems

This book is made possible in part by a donation by Lenny Schneir in the name of feminist author and artist Merlin Stone.

Copies of this book have been purchased with funding in part from the Root Family for distribution to Volusia County schools as part of the Volusia County Poet Laureate's Young Poets Mentoring Program.

Thanks to Yuyutsu Sharma for his editorial assistance in publishing this book.

Thanks to my friends, the fine poet Adam Fisher, to my wife Sandy for loving me, and my kids—Jessica, Emily, Daniel and Aileen—for making me proud and happy.

Nirala Series
ALL VOWS

David B. Axelrod is Volusia County, Florida Poet Laureate and before that, was Suffolk, Long Island Poet Laureate. A self-proclaimed "populist" poet, his mission is to promote the appreciation and writing of poetry. He performs at and sponsors numerous public events, and has established a Young Poets Mentoring Program. By making his poetry accessible and his performances lively, he hopes to encourage greater creativity, literacy and a love of literature. Dr. Axelrod holds a University of Massachusetts B.A. in English; an M.A. in poetry from The Johns Hopkins University Writing Seminars; a University of Iowa Writing Workshop M.F.A. in poetry, and a Ph.D. in not-for-profit program design and administration from Union Institute. His poems have been translated into and published in fifteen languages in hundreds of periodicals, and in twenty-two books of poetry. He is the recipient of three Fulbright Awards, including being the first official Fulbright Poet-in-Residence in the People's Republic of China. He has shared the stage with such notables as Robert Bly, Allen Ginsberg, Louis Simpson and Galway Kinnell, and performed at the United Nations and for the American Library Association. He is also a well-known arts administrator, founder and director of 3WS World Wide Writers Services, founder of and still an officer in Writers Unlimited Agency, Inc., and is publisher of Writers Ink Press. Dr. Axelrod is Director of the Creative Happiness Institute, Inc., and lives with his wife, Sandy, in Daytona Beach, Florida. His website is www.poetrydoctor.org, and he can be reached by emailing axerlod@poetrydoctor.org.

BY THE SAME AUTHOR

Poetry

Stills from a Cinema (1968, 1971)
Starting from Paumanok (1972)
Myths, Dreams and Dances (1974)
A Dream of Feet (1976)
A Meeting with David B. Axelrod
and Gnazino Russo (1979)
The Man Who Fell in Love With a Chicken (1980)
Home Remedies: New and Selected Poems (1982)
The End of the Universe (1987)
White Lies (1988)
Resurrections (1989)
A Perpetual Calendar of Poems (1989)
Love in the Keys (1991, 2nd Edition, 2001)
The Universal Language (1993)
The Chi of Poetry (1995)
Random Beauty (2001)
Another Way (2005, 2nd Edition, 2014)
The Impossibility of Dreams (2007)
Deciduous Poems (2008)
How to Apologize (2009)
The SPEED Way: NASCAR Poems
(2011, 2nd Edition 2014)
Rusting: Ways to Keep Living (2014)

Biography

Merlin Stone Remembered (2014)

David B. Axelrod

ALL VOWS

New and Selected Poems

Introduction by
George Wallace

Nirala

Nirala Publications
G.P.O. Box 7004
Munish Plaza, Ansari Road,
Daryaganj, New Delhi-110002
niralabooks@yahoo.co.in

niralapublications.com

———

First Edition 2017

———

ISBN 81-8250-082-6

———

Copyright © 2017 David B. Axelrod

———

Cover Design: Shailendra Saxena

———

Cover Art: Copyright © 2017 Jessica Robinson

———

Printed at
Chaman Offset Press
New Delhi-2

Contents

Preface / 11
Introduction / George Wallace / 13

This Is a Happy Poem / 19
Random Beauty / 20
Disappearance / 21
Seeing Things as They Are / 22
The Reoccurring Metaphor / 23
On Reading *A Brief History of Time* / 24
Thanks to Doppler / 26
For the Valentine I Don't Have / 27
Nearing the End / 28
The Slaughter / 29
"We Need What We Want"/ 30
Not Fighting / 31
Philosophical Differences / 32
Like Flowers / 33
Girl at a Sidewalk Café / 34
Eating Their Hearts Out / 35
Watching You / 36
I Want to Be With You / 37
Kissing in Front of the Microwave / 38
It's a Happy Man / 39
Resurrections / 40
Code Blue / 42
His Leaving / 44
Near Death / 46
Shrinking / 47
He Was Calm / 48
Widows / 49
For Gail, Who Called Herself "Charlie" / 50
Elegies for My Family / 52

We Are All Hit and Run / 54
Steve Comes Back / 56
Old Age Can Be Heroic / 58
Nanny and Zayde / 59
David, My Namesake, My Father / 60
At Simpson's Reading / 61
Pickling / 62
Robert Frost / 63
Real Poetry / 64
Seeing the Specialist / 65
Two Sonnets in Fear of Cancer
The Odds Makers / 66
Through Sickness / 67
The Vandal / 68
Heroics / 69
Four for the Kids
Smell My Fingers / 70
Cat Walk / 70
The Pro / 71
The Lifetime Channel / 71
For His Son / 73
Mother and Child / 74
Parenting / 75
White Lies / 76
The Small-Fry Club / 77
The Pile On / 78
Bullied / 79
Faith / 80
Class Clown / 82
S O S / 83
Whistling / 84
Peg Leg Bates / 85
The Critical Weakness / 86
Gimme Culture / 87
The Closest I've Come to Being Normal / 88
The Full Moon / 89
A Guide to Suburban Birds / 90
Bird Understandings / 91
Misjudgments / 92
The Buddhist Bird / 93
Torrey Pines, California / 94

Spring the Age-Old Question / 95
Campsite, Eraclea-Minoa, Sicily / 96
Beach Countdown / 97
Weather Patterns / 98
November / 99
Midwinter, Stony Brook Harbor / 100
A Single Heron / 101
Autographs / 102
Wishing / 103
One for My Father / 104
The Last Time My Father Beat Me / 105
Honor Thy Father / 106
Curiosity / 107
Fingering / 108
Celebrate Good Times / 110
Seder in the Jewish Nursing Home / 111
Caution: Cancer Causes Poetry / 112
½ Scientist, ½ Woman / 113
Curing Rilke / 114
The Savior / 115
The Dirty Old Man / 116
Alone in Your House / 118
Clorox Clean / 119
From Such Meditations / 120
Meditation on My MGB / 121
The Snowbird's Sonnet / 122
Sun Worship / 123
Florida Haikus and Tankas / 124
In Favor of a New Poet Laureate / 127
The End of the Universe / 128
The Man Who Fell in Love With His Chicken / 129
A Lesson in Friendship / 130
Tongue Hotel / 131
For the Birds / 132
Animal Truths / 134
Cockroach Immortality / 135
The Myth of Mathematics / 136
Soccer / 137
Hoop Dreams / 138
Little League / 139
Dry-Mouth Syndrome / 140

Forgive and Forget / 141
The South Still Rises / 142
Shooting Doves / 143
Cop Story / 146
Heritage / 148
Prejudice / 150
Guilty / 151
Black Friends / 152
Homeless / 154
On Being Safe / 155
Calling Out Their Names / 156
The Suffering Goes Both Ways / 158
A Short Course on the Holocaust / 160
All Vows / 161
Once in a While a Protest Poem / 162
Why I Cut My Barber / 163
Mandatory Reporting / 164
Surprises / 166
The Dead Have No Respect / 167
Contact Myth / 168
Downcast / 169
Day Breaks / 170
Speech Therapy / 171
Child's Play / 172
Caged / 173
Climate of Our Disposition / 174
Dark Thoughts / 175
Betrayal Is Better Served / 176
Dear Mary-Ann / 177
Politics in Four Beats / 178
Even Diamonds Melt / 180
Late Train Out of Manhattan / 181
Censorship / 182
Duty / 184
Weapon of Choice / 185
Fifty Fifty / 186
Foreseeing Change / 187
Morning Songs / 188

Preface

E ven before I became a County poet laureate, I regarded myself as a populist poet and author. I spent thirteen years as a full-time college student acquiring numerous degrees, during which time I learned a great deal about poetry and literature, but what I appreciated most were the chances to meet teachers and authors who spoke to me directly. Some professors study the science of literature—preoccupied with literary devices and vocabulary. Others see poetry as a riddle to be solved. What I enjoyed most, and wish to emulate, is writing that is meant to communicate. I'm all for experiment and invention. The best writers show us what we otherwise might have overlooked and do so by using vibrant language. But I prefer meaning over manipulation of forms, imagery over excessive metaphor. Perhaps I've traded complexity for a love of humanity but I'll go with my friend and critic George Wallace, who says in his introduction to my work that I am "sometimes deceptively artless." I would be sad if I were "artless," but the deception here is the key. I've put a lifetime into making it look easy—easy enough that I can bring many more people into the world of poetry.

Before I assembled the poems in this book, I collected all my published work into one continuous manuscript hundreds of pages long. From those pages I've selected poems that could serve as subject-matter prompts and models for others to try their hand at writing poetry. I thought of Tennyson who revised his poetry in his later life, which critics say did not improve it. But my task was not to rewrite. Rather, I also wanted to test my work against a newer measure I have imposed on myself—whether my poems are "important." I would like to think that a good poem is transpersonal—calling attention to things sad or joyous that actually matter to those who experience the words. I would ask you to think about the purpose of poetry. I hope my poems are of use. Perhaps they will be important to you. I'd be very happy if you were so comfortable with my work that you created poems of your own.

—David B. Axelrod
Daytona Beach, Florida

Introduction

In the novel *Life and Times of Alexis Zorbas*, Nikos Kazantzakis' eponymous character declares "clever people and grocers—they weigh everything." That's something poet David B. Axelrod has a thing or two to say about. "Honeysuckle is its own revelation, its sweetness the perfect perfume," he writes. Axelrod, always the teacher, is more fundamentally, the poet who time and again illustrates how to go beyond weighing, and become our own revelation.

Clover, with its "perfect crown," doesn't need a reason. "A Single Heron," with an eye for the silver flash and a natural instinct to "swallow life whole," doesn't ask why. A bird "knows how to die." What, Axelrod asks us, are the sour-mouthed constructs and customs of religions and societies compared to an oil guy sitting in the cab of his delivery truck in the winter sun, tilting back his bottle of Orange Crush?

"We know the suchness of routine:
piecework, patchwork, low-paid jobs;
mindless work with no reward."

In the world according to Axelrod—the natural world and the social human world—there are lessons to be learned beyond the profane, if you pay attention to the fundamentals. Not always sacred lessons, but excellent ones for all that—revealing themselves to be, with startling regularity, hints and suggestions concerning important ways and means we well might emulate.

In Axelrod's world, individuals tug somewhat at their relationships with each other, but the relationships endure. Bodies slow and stiffen, but they endure too—and mostly work. And yes, it's a world darkened by the pervasive presence of societal injustice, and his "gut burns with the acid" of it all—but he's also "addicted to the pain." There is a self-reflexive tendency in all this, a metapoesis, part Chaplin, part Pushkin, and part visionary. Because in his most transcendent moments an Axelrod poem—having done with its accounting—sees behind the mechanical veil of rules and religions, and discovers that there are big wheels turning.

Poem by poem, Axelrod offers up an accountancy of the spirit which runs against the grain and wakes us up. "I'm not teaching English," he declares, "I'm teaching empathy." In the individual poems there is a palpable resurrection of the particularity of the moment. And in the aggregate, the reader is offered a richly variegated compendium of moments. Dizzyingly so. But the poems hold fast to a sextant more true than any fixed point of land. In a manner sometimes prankish, sometimes frank—sometimes deceptively artless—Axelrod invites us to travel with him, drawing moment from the littlest of things, and from the great.

An Axelrod poem is a moment itself, aware of itself, not always processing that awareness comfortably but always delivering of itself with a wry intelligence that defies uncertainty, and lies somewhere between a shrug and a smirk. One thing about the man—he bounces back. And having done so, invites us to bounce back too.

"Sure, I'm hurting, but nothing

extreme, nothing eviscerating.
It seems like a good time
to share a laugh with you."

Face facts. It would be nice to be an Axelrod poem.
Because an Axelrod poem gets up off the canvas,
squares itself up, and declares itself to go another
round. "Foreseeing Change" tells us Kabbalists
hold their mysteries, Daoists hold their yarrow
sticks. David Axelrod holds tight to relation-
ships—doomed or delightful—spell-casting nor-
malities of interaction that are triumph and trauma
rolled up into a ball and thrown against a garage
door for fun.

Once in a while he exercises a propensity for self-
deception. "Life without that special someone is
just fine," lies an Axelrod protagonist, probably
to himself. "The sun still shines, the crocuses find
their way to spring." We know right off the bat
where that ball's headed—Trouble. Life's trouble,
says Zorba, only death is not. Or as Axelrod puts
it, "we need each other to holler at or slowly drive
each other mad." Life has its moments, he dec-
lares, when we leap into the surfy froth and "kiss
like Neptune." But more often than not, Axelrod
offers us moments when we fail. Fingers stiffen,
knuckles calcify, and then one day we are done.
The ineluctable hand of mortality reaches into our
pockets and steals the "gold watch." Even in "One
for My Father," there is no Kaddish, no fancy fu-
neral, no year of earthly prayers.

Earth is "a washerwoman with a sponge," ready to
wipe the slate clean of whatever has died or dims.
Earth leaves us "Clorox Clean," our fingerprints
burned off, bleached to the knee and sole. But when
all is said and done, beauty—random beauty—
transcends. It is through assertions such as these
that David Axelrod betrays himself as a romantic.
Sort of. Comfortably uncomfortable in both this

world and the next. Ready for anything, wearing "a bathing suit and a woolen hat."

We find him standing before a rusted old MG with a ballpeen hammer and a can of Bondo. "I'm stupid," he admits, with a poetic grin. "I still love the sun, luxuriating in my backyard with a book and iced tea … Nobody can tell me Vitamin D stands for death."

We find him standing in a meditation room, immersed in the scent of sandalwood. "Pay attention," says Axelrod. When Rilke says he fears that if his devils leave him, his angels will as well, pay attention. When modern medicine offers no real answer, just pills to forget, pay attention. Pay attention. Breathe deeply. "Breathe slowly, shoulders drooping." Just be there, with or without the others who surround us. "Be glad you are alive."

Like a wading bird on a heron-priested shore. Like a clover with its perfect crown. Like … like Zorba, who knows that sometimes you have to cut the rope of human logic which enslaves you, and just dance.

"This is the medicine
we all seek, the power that we have.
We dream to find it."

Welcome to the poetry of David B. Axelrod. Be glad you are holding this book in your hands.

—**George Wallace**
May 10, 2016

ALL VOWS
New and Selected Poems

"David holding Daniel" by Jessica Robinson (1984)

This Is A Happy Poem

Not all la la pixie dust
but okay, things are good.
My Ma said she just wanted
to live long enough to see me
well. I was a sickly little kid,
and a ninety-pound teenage
weakling. Now, I visit the gym
though one trainer told me,
"Muscle mass decreases
at your age." Mostly, my
parts are working if a tad
more slowly. My hearing is
definitely dimmer. My joints
are stiff, but I ain't dead yet.
So many friends and family
have departed. And that
brings me back to "happiness,"
which I'm content to define
as "the absence of pain." Sure,
I'm hurting, but nothing
extreme, nothing eviscerating.
It seems like a good time
to share a laugh with you.

Random Beauty

Some can't admit the randomness of beauty,
as if a clover's perfect crown should need
a reason. Others see Gods at work in every
season, heroes personified in stars.
I have a quarrel with religion, imposing
order on things better left alone.
Honeysuckle is its own revelation,
its sweetness the perfect perfume.
I'll take chaos over counting angels—
columbine, clematis, abundant
at roadside. Who needs Deuteronomy
or Numbers? Beauty transcends all laws.

Disappearance

1.

I considered the phoenix—
into the fire, a quick release
of gas, the efficacy of ash.
But does one truly rise?
Is it a spirit or a conscious
recollection of the past?

2.

Those who acknowledge
nothing swim comfortably
in the dark. The salt of
their mother floats them.
The mulch of their father
awaits them when they pass.

3.

Some believe resurrection,
others in coming back.
Whether I die slowly or
fast, make sure I burn.
I'm good with that. Afterlife,
memorials, are of no concern.

Seeing Things As They Are

It started with my eyes, framed
in a rear-view mirror, staring
at me—so much older than
the driver rushing toward some
self-appointed task—shopping,
meetings, dinner with whom?
Some say there are old souls—
small children who know more
than they should. I saw the backhand
of abuse, the fist of prejudice, long
before I aged. Now, it's my hands
that scare me. I study them as I reach
to adjust the rear-view mirror—
with their liver spots, stiff knuckles,
skin stretched thin over piano-wire
tendons. Don't blame me if I'm
forced to look away. There's no
sense in looking back.

The Reoccurring Metaphor

The snap of the metal cage
still startles me though I've
sprung this door before.
I couldn't resist sniffing,
finding an entrance.
I walked in happily, heedless
of the trigger on the floor.
Trapped, I beat against
the bars. Banging my head
brings a small trickle of blood,
a reassuring pain. No more
freedom. No need for self-
control. I can only relieve
myself and live in my own fear.

On Reading
'A Brief History of Time'

(For Stephen Hawking.)

1. Ancient Wisdom

(Hawking says, "If you meet your anti-self, don't shake hands. You would both vanish in a great flash of light.")

To name the beast is to know it.
If you meet a monster, call it
by its name. Offer it your hand.
Better to create that flash
of light than slaughter and decay.

2. Old Time Religion

(In quantum physics, the speed of light is absolute.)

Aquinas asserted there is a God
and then said that he'd proved it.

Einstein declared light was absolute
and no one could destroy it.

Koheleth whispered
the vanity of human wishes.

3. Same Story, Different Day

(The term "quark" derives from a cryptic passage from James Joyce: "Three quarks for Muster Marks!")

Call heaven "quark," hell "antiquark,"
their meeting "annihilation."
So Armageddon is retold
and physics explains creation.

4. A Doppler Love Poem

(By the Doppler Effect we can tell the universe is constantly expanding. However, there are "singularities" wherein all logic fails.)

As I view you through this telescope
of time, your hair becomes more red —
your waves less frequent and as
your distance from me grows,
I am more blue, as if rushing
toward you. Doppler knew
that both of these could not
at once be true but we all know
in love there is no logic.

Thanks To Doppler

Nothing passed ancient observers
rapidly enough for them to notice
a change in pitch. Sounds came
at them as if the air were angry,
signaling something likely
dangerous, and once passed,
one could heave a sigh of relief.
We had to wait for fast conveyances,
sirens blaring, or trains with obligatory
whistles sounding, before Doppler
noticed: first, a rising pitch; then
as quickly, a falling off.
He calculated the compression
of waves, the consequent higher
frequency, the corollary stretching
out and lowering pitch of objects
moving away. He even applied
this to the movement of the stars.
Thus, reassured, when blaring
somewhere raises our attention,
forcing us to calculate whether
it is coming or going, or when
a race car roars by us, its fierce
shriek subsiding, we can thank
Doppler, not to mention that
the monster did not eat us.

For The Valentine I Don't Have

Life without that special someone
is just fine. The sun still shines,
the crocuses find their way to spring.
The house is warm. Out walking
through the mall, I don't need anything.
Grown kids are plenty to contend with—
even if they don't ask, I buy them gifts.
There's a grandchild, a sign of hope.
But I'm no dope. Perhaps it's the happy
arguments I'm missing, perhaps
the kissing. On days like this,
I find the lack of you distressing.

Nearing The End

"I hate you," she whispered
just loudly enough that it
woke him. Each time he
asked, "What did you say?"
she denied saying anything.
This time he sat bolt upright
at the edge of the bed and froze.
It took her a minute. Was she
waiting for his usual inquiry?
"Are you okay?" she asked.
He willed his own paralysis,
even slowed his breathing.
"Are you okay?" she persisted,
and reached for his shoulder.
He considered the will to live
and willingness to die. "Yes,"
he uttered, allowing her to
lower him back to their
pillows. "It isn't the death
of me," he told himself,
"It's simply time to go."

The Slaughter

Rain's gentle revolver riddles our sleep.
Wet tongue of lightening
dark growl of thunder
bullets through our dreams.
A hand to find a crease of flesh
unconscious fingers probing,
a skinning that starts with a slit.
And no one minds the trembling limbs
as the hide is peeled. Some are born
for love, others for the slaughter.

Penitent rain. Cleansing rain.
Sorry rain. Satiating rain.
All these things we do that lovers do:
begging you, licking you
bathed in tears, chilling fears.
Wake with a rapping at the window,
an arm in a clinch around you.
Tonight there'll be no recriminations.
Only the soft spatter of water
as the flesh is trimmed from the bone.

"We Need What We Want"

(An observation by René Dubos.)

We need each other to holler
at or slowly drive each other
mad, repeating lists of things
to do and all we want: like you,
ticking the piano off to an irregular
Anna Magdalena Bach; getting
minisculely better every day
you drive me from the house
to let you practice. Or me
practicing poems on the IBM,
impossible to speak to before,
during or when I'm done.

We need what we want: we
want a single day the garbage
cans empty themselves, groceries
are shopped for automatically.
We want the earnings of Getty,
uncorrupted; a list of things
that reads like poetry; the carefree
life; sex without responsibility;
the way to live with grace and art;
a graceful way to die. We
need each other.

Not Fighting

1.
These arguments we have are not
fights, not even disagreements
but hauntings from our pasts—
the who-we-weres and what-was-
done-to-us that bubble up, though
we know we shouldn't raise our
voices or take that creepy stance that
says, "I'm the boss," or "I must be
right." Facts need not be litanies,
as if dignity were a debate, or trust
on trial. "Why are you shouting at me?"
"Why do you use that tone of voice?"

2.
Freud entered the ring, analyzing
every nuance from our baby past.
Jung wrestled archetypes of male
dominance and female submission.
Behaviorists, short of time, counselled
us to set up cues: "When you say that,
it pushes my button." Better just
agree, whatever angry words, we
are not fighting—just letting
the ghosts out for a talk. Later,
a light caress can push them back
into the hurt past we have forgotten.

Philosophical Differences

The backseat driver sits
by my side applying
the brakes, cautioning,
"There's a car!" which,
by the way, is ten car
lengths ahead at a corner
and I am already fully
aware. "Here are the keys,"
I offer, stopped at the roadside,
"Would you prefer to drive?"
But now, she is offended,
says she just wants to help,
so I drive on. "Watch out,"
she tells me, loudly enough
for my heart to pound.
I will learn to ignore her,
more ready for death than
she, who holds onto life with
white knuckles while I am
just here for the ride.

Like Flowers

I bought Prudence a purple orchid
pinned to her taffeta for the prom.
Judy was a Himalayan poppy
who secretly made me high.
Gail was a red rhododendron
blooming by my door.
Ellie was lavender foxglove,
and Mary, a Kennedy rose.
There was one wife like belladonna
and another like a bleeding heart.
Sandy is my purple tulip
I cultivate to see her bloom.

Girl At A Sidewalk Cafe

(A picture that Renoir might paint.)

You sit with sunlight
through your hair.
The sailors eat their cockle
stew. The sailors sit and look
at you—the accent of the light
and dark across your legs held
just apart, your chest exposed
until breasts part, the sunlight
streaming through your thighs.
The sailors with their fishy
sighs, their passion dilating
their eyes; they climax as they
look at you (schools of fishes
cross their thighs). They pay
the waitress for the stew.
The sunlight playing with your
dress accents the contours of
your breasts. The sailors eat
their mutton pie and wait until
the sea is dry, and so you sit
and satisfy a hundred tourists
passing by, and every sailor seated
there, netted by your sunlit hair.

Eating Their Hearts Out

She barely ate: a muffin
for breakfast; little else
all day. She said she hadn't
made love to her husband
for a year (half portions
of plain fish for supper
no potatoes) who'd gone
into mourning for his
mother and even before
wanted no children.
She said she was content
with abstinence.

Her lover ate voraciously:
steak and fries and bacon
for breakfast. His marriage
he said even his friends
called heroic (all afternoon
sweets, supper seven courses)
and his wife made love like
a ritual so even when it was
good it wasn't. That's why he
said he could never get enough.

Together for a tryst, they tried
the local bistros. He cut down on
desserts. She bucked up and ate.
They made a feast of love.

Watching You

I spent till sunrise
watching you your
restless breaths
your high-boned face
your nakedness
defined in blue-gray
light of quarter moon.
You sighed and turned
and still I stared
the thick curled knot
of jet-black hair
tied up to bare
a soft strong neck
supple shoulders
the outline
of small breasts.

Until you turned
again toward me
eyes flickering
in half-surprise.
I spent till sunrise
watching you
protector of your
dreams and sighs.

I Want To Be With You

(For Harold and Dolores, April, 1966.)

I want to be with you
in all times of day:
cool pink milkmanned mornings
when streets are disguised
by the angle of the sun;
and days when the air is
sliced by rain we can
chase the currents
sluicing over streets.
And then, I want to walk
exactly straight across
deserted parks guided by
a parallax of lamp poles
when the ground is frozen
to the vasting sky by absolutes
of cold. I'll steal a grocery cart
and you climb in. I'll push you
to my world and you'll come in.
I want to make a list of hours
we can share and search for them
forever.

Kissing In Front
Of The Microwave

Kissing in front
of the microwave
set on high
for two minutes
your arms around
my waist
mine
curled behind
your back
a buzzing
in our ears
the temperature
rising
one loud bell
a rapid boil.

It's A Happy Man

It's a happy man who can
make love on a Monday morning.
So many pieces to the heart:
the right woman of course,
who desires not just to lie abed
pretending Sunday, but lusts
for love, ready to smile, humid with
the thought. And work, whatever
tools await—skillet or screwdriver,
computer with its tactile grin—he
would need at least a forgiving boss
who didn't stand pointing at a watch,
grimacing at lateness. Then, there's
the very bed, a sea of slippery silk,
though hay alone is legendary.
The clock need not alarm. Instead,
a gentle hand wrapping around,
stroking a belly, arriving at a breast.
You can imagine the rest.
This poem is about a happy man
not sex. And he, floating on his lover's
raft, sights a misty island where they
both can live without deadlines,
bosses, traffic that strangles or mon-
etary chills that freeze the best
man's assets. Not a word, just love
with a happy woman who sends
her man to battle satisfied.

Resurrections

In my dream, I put my hands up,
my head back, dive toward the sky,
rising to the other world, thinking,
this is the magic we all have,
the power that we seek.

The unshaven man on the corner,
dressed in filthy dungarees, ragged
work shirt, a cardboard sign, "Help
Me," aimed at cars stopped at a light;
he seeks the power.

The old man lying on the tight-sheeted
hospital bed, bare skin exposed beneath
a half-opened cotton johnny, bony hand
pressed to his temple; he seeks the power.

The sixteen-year-old girl, panicking
on the birthing table, crying as they
prepare her, her ankles tied,
a mystery inside; she seeks the power.

I rise slowly, press my back against
smooth plaster walls, raise my hands to dive,
see the light above and yearn for it.
Suddenly, terrified, I fight to keep my
feet down. "Hold me," I call my wife,
asleep beside me. "Hold me down or
I will die." Awakened by my cry, she

reaches round me: "I'm here, I have you."
Anchored fast, I remember what I've dreamed
and watch my wife fall back to sleep;
listen as her breathing deepens.

Next day, I tell my friend my dream —
my fear of disappearing. He says
the right hand holds the power, sends it
to the left. Circling his palm over my head,
he calms me. He is Abenaki, Native
American, grows his own food,
studies the seasons. It's late March
and he asks me to watch him tap
the sugar maples on forty acres
passed to his hands, ancestral lands.
Standing behind his house, we feel
the syrup flowing through thawing
roots and leave the earth, welcoming
what is sweet within us.

That night, my wife says she is sick,
stomach uneasy. I place my right hand
over her belly, my left just at her
side to make a circuit; tell her what
I've learned. Does she believe me?
No need to hear her say — the energy
a rush of heat between us and she
is cured. This is the medicine
we all seek, the power that we have.
We dream to find it.

Code Blue

So the doctor left it written on my chart:
"pain killers on demand" — a junkie's dream.
I'm in the hospital — a skin graft on my leg.
It's 9 p.m. I've read a hundred pages of Saul
Bellow's *Herzog*. I've watched TV. I'm bored.
I push the button for the nurse and ask
for something. What harm in getting stoned,
drifting numbly off to sleep? I roll over,
pull a corner of my pajamas down
the same way I've gotten all the other shots.

"No," nurse says when she returns.
"Here's where it's done," and she rolls
me back to grasp my arm, find a vein,
sting me as she pushes the needle in.
She leaves me with a wad of alcohol-
soaked cotton compressed in the crux
of my arm.

        So what happens next?
I die. I feel myself fading —
can barely push the button
for the nurse. All I remember is
floating in the room, looking down
through a circle of heads, people
in white robes, wondering if they
were angels. Someone ashen white
is lying on a stretcher. Someone
is counting, "60 over 40, 60 over

40. Damn! We've lost his pulse again.
He's dead."

      I realize
the person I see is me.
"Wait a minute," I say. "I'm here,"
and instantly I'm on the stretcher;
hear them counting "30 over 10,
40 over 20, 60 over 40. We've
got a pulse again." I sleep for fifteen
hours.

      When I awake, I ask
a different nurse what happened.
"We went code blue with you,"
she says. "You should have seen
them running from every corner
of the hospital." "You mean I
fainted?" I ask. "Oh no," she laughs,
we gave you up for dead. We tried
adrenaline, the paddles. Just when
we quit, your heart began to beat again."

His Leaving

He begged me not to make him go.
He told me, "Hospitals are for dying,"
so I watched him wince, walking
with a cane, clearly suffering.
But when the fever hit, I insisted.
"Sepsis," the doctor said. "from
a fissure in his intestines." I saw his
frantic eyes grow dim as the poison
spread, and then coma. I couldn't even
lie to him about recovery. The last words
I spoke into his parchment stare,
"Your wife and daughter love you."
The bedside monitor quickened
for a moment before he died—though
the nurse doubted that he heard me.
He always was a tough guy, seasoned
Marine, trained to ignore pain. To prove
what? His wife begged him to get help,
but it was I who promised, "You'll be
alright. I won't let you die," and kept
a bedside vigil. As if I had that power.
At the funeral, his wife cursed him
for leaving, threw a stone into his grave
that echoed off the coffin. That night,
his voice came to me accusingly, "You
let me die." I protested my innocence
but for days he wouldn't leave me.
Determined, I took him with me

to the beach in the dark of night,
and though the rules said strictly
not to, I built a little fire. "You
have to go," I pleaded as the yellow
flame of salted wood sent sparks
into the sky. From my pocket I
took a paper and wrote his name,
placed it in the fire. The page
flashed to light grey ash, carried
skyward toward the sea. "It's time,
good friend. I'll help your family."
Suddenly, a breeze stirred, first
in the nearby palms, then carried
down the beach toward me. "Go
ahead," I said. "You'll be okay."
And just like that, I sensed him
drift away.

Near Death

(A sonnet for Aaron Kramer.)

"Do not go gentle?" Dylan missed the mark;
as if we all must think of death as dark.
I think that death's more gentle than a birth.
I've seen a light that glows beyond the earth;
but not a heaven, not Elysian Fields.
One needn't find salvation; rather, yield
to that same light that little children miss
in nurseries where doting parents kiss
their fears away indulgently. But why?
Suppose it isn't fear that makes kids cry
but yearning for the prebirth light they left.
Then go, good journeyman, gently cleft.
Greet death as quietly as candles burn.
From light you came. To light
      you shall return.

Shrinking

"I've accepted my mortality,"
he says, eyes toward the floor,
even as he thinks, "Maybe
a year more to live." After all,
they've told him it is a slow-
growing cancer. But he is thinner,
ever thinner and paler, and he has
replaced, "See you soon," with,
"See you if I'm up to it." Actuarially,
he says he's right on target for a white,
non-smoking male. "Seventy-five,
that's about all we get, but, personally,
it doesn't seem like enough." His son,
in Seattle, has asked him to move so
he won't die alone. "Thanks for listening
to my case history," he says. "You know,
I was trained as a shrink to listen to other
people's troubles." He pauses, "'Shrink'
always sounded pejorative to me. Now,
that's all I have left to do. For all their
ministrations, I'll have less strength
each day until the end."

He Was Calm

(A MacArthur air controller describing the pilot of a small plane lost off Fire Island, February, 1972: "He was calm almost until the end when he began asking for his wife.")

Asleep with the automatic
pilot on after an extra hour
in the air, darker
when you awoke than ever
the sea had seemed
and infinitely cold and empty.
You talked to the tower, asked
for coordinates, believed
in landings. Small planes
on overland routes don't
carry rafts; you didn't have
a flashlight; you thought of home
and where you'd left it. A light
to aim at—a ship—six thousand
feet of altitude to average
over fifteen miles of ocean.
Your calculations broke your
faith, ringing in the air controller's
ears and couldn't they
do something to preserve the human
voice, phone-patch you to your wife?
Instead, a claxon signal of the crash,
the hiss of water.

Widows

Widows
left with only tinted
portraits of the past
and tinted
hair combed thin
as life to frame
their worn complexions
keep
their homes by
taking strangers into
memories-of-children-
haunted
rooms.
Left to feign
the youth that withered
long ago, they
wheeze
a friend hello
while walking to the store
or talk on porches
to impatient tenants
just to hear a human voice.
Lonely women
cobwebs in their wombs
live by taking strangers
into their rooms.

For Gail, Who Called Herself "Charlie"

You say you are an exotic
dancer, brag how good you are,
rubbing yourself against
the wooden rails that separate
your bright spot of stage
from the small Formica
tabletops where guys
mostly in their twenties
chug beers and cheer you on.
"I tease them, let them
tuck fives and tens in my
G-string. If I go bottom-
less, I get them good
and hot. That's when
I really get a lot.
I drive them wild."

Your shoulders stiffen
as you talk, your jaw
thrust forward like an
angry child. "Come down
and watch me." Your eyes
dance in a sideward glance;
the open buttons of your
baggy shirt an invitation.

And now there is no chance
to see you on the circuit,

your hips pumping frustration
into every bastard
in the bar. Your long
brown hair that whipped
you as you whirled
is stilled. Your try-
to-catch-me eyes are
closed; your half-smile,
a tight-lipped, eternal
grimace. OD-ed at twenty-one.
How far away from everyone
you've danced, as if death
alone could be exotic.

Elegies: For My Family

One man bursts his liver with a bottle,
the alcohol fine slivers rushing
through the blood. He bleeds until
it kills him, colored yellow for
the wake, a bit of rouge for emphasis.
He is still forty when they bury him.

Then the woman with the tumorous
brain moves in. Somewhere, she thinks,
she is pregnant, cells growing in her mind
in spherical, thin-layered zygote, pulsing
with life, displacing her vision (it blurs
and she is crying); making her left arm
numb (her fingers clutch and release
the yellow cotton nightgown). She
is concerned about her hair, a glossy
black; it will fall out from radiation.
The coffin closed, they save themselves
a wig. She was a comely thirty-eight.

But the old man, ninety-three, is loudest
when he pisses; congestive—his kidneys
lazy and his heart—a catheter to drain
him; a surprise for the nurses when
he gets it up as they adjust him.
A character he is, and old enough
you'd think, but never satisfied.
He dies in his sleep with a smile,
his fingers on his peep.

What is all this clockwork ticking
in our bodies stuffed like pipe
bombs with crude electric fuses?
The alarm is set, a ring that wakes
and kills us. We live however many
years just waiting to explode.

We Are All Hit And Runs

1.
The deer startled, head lighted
at the roadside: I remember Jackknife,
his wife hugging him on their super
black Harley outside North Hadleyville.
Nearly midnight the coroner guessed
when the full buck leaped from the roadside
impaled on the handlebars.

2.
A heavy rain: I am riding full-throttle
down the highway when the road ahead
comes alive with small white flashing
frogs, jumping unsyncopated; hundreds
and unavoidable—plowed through
and I swear I hear their rubber skins
popping beneath the wheels.

3.
Tommy my friend, touring England
with his new wife out on a fling
turned a corner in the countryside
head on into coma.

4.
Mr. Katz, surviving twenty years pogroms,
fifteen days an Atlantic crossing,
sixty years a cobbler, at 80 years old
he met a fender of a Mustang
in Miami Beach.

5.
I tuck the seat belt around,
a harness, a way to hang
onto life; but the reins
are loose behind me. On impact.
where do we go?

Steve Comes Back

Your bull neck through the back
window of a beat up Cadillac,
seated half a head above the steering
wheel in your white painter's cap.
But you died a year ago, outside
Tampa where poverty and hope
had brought you for a short try
again at home improvements.

When your wife was dying,
you needed three thou a month
for shellfish serum someone said
would save her. Every job half done.
Get the check, pay the doctor,
run to the next paper-hanging,
partitioning, paint job. In no time,
twenty years of reliability
ruined and your wife dead.

You told the judge, "What you want
me to do?" "Pay your bills," he
reprimanded you. "The doctors take
everything. I can't pay no more."
When the judge threatened to lock
you up for contempt you laughed and left.

They never came to get you,
though your troubled daughter
got herself arrested. You dreamed
of native Naxos, Greece; packed
for Florida. In your mind, you felt
the pressure building.

They found you early in the morning
slumped over the wheel, the hood
of the '74 Caddy wrapped around
a Southern Pine. The coroner skipped
the alcohol in the blood, the accident
trauma; listed the cause of death
as a cerebral hemorrhage. How could
he know the bubble had burst long before?

Old Age Can Be Heroic

(For Philip Kransberg.)

My grandfather, when he was young
and working as a junkman, could
carry cast iron stoves across
the room, his arms spread-eagled,
the weight across his shoulders.
As he grew blindly older,
walking itself became a matter
of carrying a great burden.
Crossing a street, retired,
he passed men working
and fell until he spread
his arms to catch himself
at the armpits, into an
open grate. The men who
lifted him complained
of his weight, but he,
bruised and embarrassed,
said that he forgave them.

Nanny And Zayde

All those years of scrapping
iron, furniture, old clothes,
he saved for her in the old black
safe, combination his secret, then
on no real occasion, dressed up
in his good silk suit and bowler,
walked in the local jeweler's
to strike a deal, placed the small felt
box beside his pocket watch.
He gave her the ring that evening:
fine platinum, large diamond,
seven chips to seat it in the center.
He thought her face would shine enough
for even his weak eyes, but Nanny,
who pinched her children's toes
in discount shoes and soured herself
on stringy gedempte fleish, was adamant:
yes, it was hers; she would not return
it, never wear it, nor forgive him.
All that suffering had to be for a reason.

David, My Namesake, My Father

(For Dave Ignatow.)

Rose said the closer you were
the crueler, and wept that you
publicly declared affairs. She
gave my daughter her first gold
crayon and a love of art. You
gave me a shot—as a poet
of reckoning, but not without
a price—living by each pro-
nouncement of what you thought
was proper poetry until I just
rebelled at your advice and put-
downs. Why didn't I accept a father
could be flawed? I loved your wit,
welcomed your kindness, burned
your books and sent you ashes,
stating, "I won't be abused." My
bad. Our loss—you a loyal son,
me a benefactor. After that,
of course, we didn't speak
though for a moment—when
you sat in repose just before
one reading—I approached you
to apologize and we both knew
it would be meaningless.

At Simpson's Reading

(In the library reference section.)

In his poems he says:
"There is no such thing
as a bad life." Today
he laughs as he reads.
Over his shoulder
on library shelves:
 Encyclopedia of Social Science.
Statistical Sources.

Louis, who can be at least
two people, writing
his marvelous poems or
fussing that he isn't loved:
Womanlist. Judaica.

For now all's well.
The audience adores him.
He's loose, personable,
ready to tell the truth:
The Complete Astrology.
Holy Bible.

But who will we meet
at the reception,
kindly poet
or angry kid?

Pickling

(For Lyn Lifshin.)

You salt your food
layers thick,
spoil a fancy steak,
disguise home fries,
preserve yourself in brine
washed with coffee through
your stained teeth.
Too many tastes to mask,
too many kinds of flesh
lovingly tongued until
the flavors soured,
swallowing poison instead
of life:
spoiled fish,
tough bird,
rancid meat.
Handshakes of salt
across your plate,
finger-pinches like
surprises; slow inverted
streams of salt—
a poultice complete
with crusted edges
drying, applied inside you,
heating you in your
thirsty sleep.

Robert Frost

(At his class I took at Amherst College, spring, 1962.)

Robert Frost would sit with his
liver-spotted, thin-skinned hands
resting on his polished cotton slacks,
and I'd sit at his feet on a carpet,
young poet at a workshop,
Amherst College lounge.

We'd read our work, talk liberally
while he smiled silently
except once I slipped a poem
over his bony knee for him
to grasp, and watched until he
pushed it back to me, silently.

Later, I asked him "Did you
like it, Sir?" His face
composed of mostly rock and
Maine potatoes, his voice hoarse
as frost, he answered, "You don't
find your voice until you're forty."

Real Poetry

doesn't dwell in the universities
it's in the torn cotton jumper
of a village carver seated
on a low oak stool he's hewn
this day carving spoons
poetry fills the red clay jugs
each balanced by a woman
fetching water at the spring
it's the leather-faced herdsman
his walnut-blackened hands
holding a staff of smooth
yellow wood.

The poems of the university
require study entwined
with myth mottled
with meanings but real poetry
is the slaughter man and the calf
its body still jerking
as its coarse-haired hide
is skinned revealing
a glistening whiteness.

Seeing The Specialist

And then there was the Nazi doctor
who struck the child between the eyes
and struck the child between the eyes
and struck the child between
the eyes, and I wait,
and I wait, and I wait—
each moment another blow
so my eyes cross or close and I
stagger in my pain, and the doctor
comes again to visit for just the moment
that he chooses, with a ball-peen hammer
and a smile. Reaching to shake
my hand, he pulls me toward him,
his vice grip on my wrist. I struggle.
He is smiling all the while. He wears
a wool-tweed suit, and smells of pipe
tobacco. I see his hair is thinning,
receding to reveal a vast, unwrinkled brow.
For a moment, I feel his smile—believe it.
There are no degrees on the pastel walls.
He is not in his own carpeted office.
This is the examining room. Suddenly,
I remember for one painful second
before he strikes, and I know I will
be seen again and again by the doctor,
and I will be told, "Be glad. He
is an expert in his field."

Two Sonnets In Fear Of Cancer

1. The Odds Makers

Awakened simultaneously at one,
we argue who's to blame, whose
        cough resounds
percussive, whether health foods help prolong
one's life; count careful people still
        struck down.
We quote the facts, make odds and place
        our bets:
In WWI, one out of four was killed.
Now one in four will die a cancer death.
An hour—no sleep. The bottle rattles, pills
half gone; we drink a glass of tepid juice.
Our terrors slow their ticking, numbed
        by drugs
that stop diurnal clocks. At noon, transfused
with sugared tea, we slump behind our mugs,
ignore the nitrates bursting in our guts,
the table strewn with bacon rinds and butts.

2. Through Sickness

Crises, you never let me comfort you,
would rather sit alone in dark and cry,
as if we hadn't been together through
ten years of births or watched our
            close friends die.
To show your rage at life you call the cops,
phone threats of self-annihilation, 9-
1-1. I wake when the receiver drops.
Dazed, I find you flushed with fear and blind
with tears. You only asked them for
            protection
a guard with gun to keep the cancer out.
"Don't call again," I beg. "The cops
            will come
and get you." Then who would drive
            me crazy,
shout my fears away, or with her
            madness, fight
to wear me out enough to sleep at night?

The Vandal

He creeps to the edge of the hedges
on the darkest night, his BB gun
beneath a surplus army jacket.
This is where he went to school.
He's older now and knows the rules
and how to break them. Raising
the polished butt beside his chin
he fires, pointing at the room
where he was kept—one quick
report of well-pumped air—
and runs for it. The pellet
punctures three-eighths-inch glass,
a burst of silver petals through
the other side, one violent glass
flower for the teacher.

Heroics

(For a sixteen-year-old amputee.)

After he'd stolen fire, the Gods
chained him to a rock, tore him
apart. And Roddy, after he'd
made his leap toward light,
touched the high voltage transformer,
"His hands," his mother explained,
"were like this." She made two
welded fists, "Two chunks
of charcoal, and his arms ..."
They had to cut them off.

A month they kept him chained
in sleep until, still on a respirator,
he awoke. "Why can't they put them
back?" he asked. The day nurse pecked
at the charred skin where his coat
and shirt burned off inside the fence
where no one dared to help him.

"At this point," his mother says,
"it hasn't gotten any easier."
And the Gods—it's never mentioned
whether once they bound him
to the rock, once the bird beak began,
they simply left or stayed to watch him.

Four For The Kids

1. Smell My Fingers (For Jessica, at 6.)

Smell my fingers my daughter
says and thrusts them
at my nose. I back dive off
my chair as if the air were
poisoned. Where have they been
those sweaty things with six
years of sticky places
scenting their past? She laughs
and chases me around the room
with germicidal weapons,
insists on my surrender.
Caught, I find a pine cone
in her fist. She tells me
it is spring and that means perfume.

2. Cat Walk (For Emily, at 8.)

The cat walks into the study as if he
owns it, turns on his motor—a delight
of snores and groans—and does a cat-
walk on my desk before he settles in my
lap. My daughter, seated on the floor,
is doing homework—History and English,
Math and Science—a bag of books
that builds her biceps and her mind.
The cat jumps down to nose among
her papers, whack a soft paw at

the pencil filling workbook blanks.
We watch him at his mindless play.
Wishing we could waste our time
that way, I say, "I'd like to be a cat."
My daughter sighs, "Daddy, do we
believe in reincarnation?"

3. The Pro (For Dan, at 6.)

He stands before
a hundred grownups
("Adults," he'd say.
"Don't baby me.")
reciting poems better
than any kiddy rhymes.
"I hope you won't
let my size fool you.
I'm small but I'm serious.
All I want is
to inspire you."

4. The Lifetime Channel (For Aileen, at 7 ½.)

Lately, you've watched
"The Baby Story" day after day,
barely better than home video,
with couples attending Lamaze,
seeing the OB-GYN. You sit
through every midwife talk until,
twenty minutes in, after the quick
yelps, push-pushes, there's

a crown and, at last, a birthing.
If I sneak my own peek, you're
leaning toward each final scream.
"Why don't they show the front?
What's happening?"
"I don't know," I say,
to duck. "You do too,"
you holler. But when you also
watch "A Wedding Story,"
with its blond Barbie brides,
its Ken-ish blue-eyed grooms,
its token interracial couples,
you believe me when I say
I don't know what makes
a perfect marriage.

For His Son Who Totaled The Car Again

He calls at 5:23 a.m. from Hancock not saying
which state. "Dad, I totaled the car." Good
news, bad news. He is, after all, speaking.
"Closed my eyes a moment on a curve."

Only two years before, that beautiful
old Lincoln totaled—an impact so fierce
the frame bent in a V. He also walked away
with only bruises, even partied later.

They say trouble comes in threes. Cats have
nine lives. Men aren't friends until they've
fought over money and women. What is
the wisdom for fathers? Apples falling?

If he survives the next crash, let him
not call me. Rather, bring his bruised
body home, which I will prodigally hug—
being an errant son myself and clearly
a major role model.

Mother And Child

I kiss your belly
button bursting out like
a silver dollar for your
sixth month. Sleek and
fat you sway before me,
lure me to our conjugal bed
to use each other gently before
the final layoff.

I kiss your thighs, see
eyes staring at me from
deep inside, that wink to
say we are captured and must
pay ransom for twenty years
before we're free.

You are too sexy to be
pregnant. I am too young
to be a father. We are
too sure we need each other
to let go.

Parenting

Parenting should be letting
one's kids alone. Yes, a smack
on an ass when there's cars
whizzing by may save a child.
But letting the kid alone lets her
grow. The more it has to be
one way, the crazier for
parents and kids. Hitting
makes hitting possible.
Try whacking someone
to give them peace of mind.
"Live by my rules," is
the prelude to, "Leave."
So she comes home with
an idiot—loves his drool.
You see a big belly,
abandonment. If she doesn't
know by now, too bad.
Better buy diapers and place
them on your eyes and ears.

White Lies

There was a lie about it
not hurting and another
about all the ice cream
you could eat. They
told me they'd see me soon
and left me with a nurse.
They never told me
about the mask
or the terrible
counting backward
from ten, until
I heard, through blinding
white-mirrored light: 9
(I couldn't breathe.) 8
(I couldn't even cry.) 7
(His eyes, his mask.) 6
(Pressing on my face.) 5
(Hands holding me down.) 4
Dimmer, swimming lights.

The Small-Fry Club

Big Brother Bob Emery was
the host of a kids' show on
Boston's WEEI radio. He'd
play his ukulele and sing,
"The Grass Is Always Greener
in the Other Fellow's Yard."
There followed shaggy-dog
stories, and fables that always
ended with a suitable moral.
I'd keep my membership card
nearby, glad if I stayed home
from school to hear him. Later,
he moved to a TV show so I could
see he looked like someone's
grandpa wearing a suit and
always so polite, except the day
they left the mic on and we heard
him say, "That's it for the little
bastards for another day." He
retired after that but I wasn't
old enough so I missed him.

The Pile On

We'd play tackle football after school
a range of ages, littler kids like me
to maybe eleven. The yard by the high
school gym was foot-worn smooth, hard mud.
We'd choose up sides. I was small but sneaky;
could sidestep bigger blockers, blitzing
the quarterback, catching his arm or leg
until another kid finished the tackle.
But once they threw the ball to me
and when, to my surprise, I caught it,
first one kid caught me and then another,
until everyone piled on so that I lay
on the ground, unable to move or breathe,
and it wasn't fun anymore. After that
I learned to wrestle, squeezing
my opponents in a deadly scissors.
Once you know fear, you can inflict it.

Bullied

I see a foot pushing my briefcase
down the row but I don't want to
jump up because my homeroom
teacher will blame me, but I need
it because it's mine, and I don't
have time for this crap, only I know
it's my choice to be odd guy out
by carrying a briefcase when no one
else does, even though those fools
have to strain their arms, balancing
all their books on their hips walking
between classes and back and forth
to school and as often they drop
everything, so my method is more
logical not to mention the briefcase
was a gift my grandma gave me and
I love its shiny, black leather, which
is waterproofed should it rain as I
walk home from junior high, except
these idiots aren't going to stop until
I beg for it back, and even if I get it
back, by then I'll be late for class,
the teacher will blame me, something
ugly could be inside with my homework,
or my homework could be missing
or torn like I'd like to do to their throats
except I'm the lone wolf and they
are the pack that's out to get me.

Faith

In the third grade
the new girl's name
was Faith Bigalow.
She had long brown hair,
brown eyes and though
I know she never wore
lipstick or rouge, her
cheeks had little blush spots
and her lips were very red.
Faith was the minister's daughter
but that didn't stop me
from loving her. At nine,
I didn't dwell on ethnic prejudice.
Often as I pulled her pigtails
at recess, she barely looked at me.
In junior high, I sat behind her.
We were joined by the alphabetical
proximity of our last names.
Through the pledge of allegiance,
the principal's announcements,
home-game pep talks and the Lord's
prayer, I watched the way she'd shrug
her shoulders, smooth her hair,
smile as she turned to receive papers
passing from the back of the room.
For our eighth-grade graduation,

I told her that I loved her
and asked her to the prom.
She said her father was assigned
to a new church so she'd
be moving soon. If you meet
her, or her sister Prudence,
please let Faith know I miss her
and for all these years I've wished
that I kissed her goodbye.

Class Clown

School is never out for the class clown.
The costume is permanent—a cock's
comb of quick puns and flippant
comments; a motley of smiles
and runs up to slap a back or grab
an ass. Ha ha. It isn't easy pasting on
that smile, keeping them laughing.
It was my favorite teacher,
consoling me that I wasn't invited
to speak at an assembly, who told me,
"If they give a nut a microphone
he might tell the truth." Leave it to me,
the jester, to tell the king, "You're naked."
Only, why, to this day, do I feel like
I'm the one left standing in the cold?

SOS

When I learned Morse Code,
the military and ham radio still
used it. Everyone knew S O S
but few needed it. My house
looked out to sea from Beverly,
past Salem toward Marblehead
harbor and our second-floor porch
was my perch, a captain's bridge,
the wheelhouse. I saw small boats
heading in and out, a large barge
towing toward channel dredging.
Something seized me—the need
for adventure, the quest for rescue.
I waited for dark, went inside to find
our brightest flashlight, and signaled:

- - - . . . - - -

- - - . . . - - -

- - - . . . - - -

Dark nights render distance difficult
to measure, so soon, a larger boat—
from its searchlight, likely the Coast
Guard—crossed quickly out of the bay.
Someone had seen my signal, called
the authorities, and though it was
impossible anyone would ever catch me,
I crouched low, all but crawled inside
and haven't confessed my folly until today.

Whistling

It was the song of a sickly kid,
my single note wheezed through
the night. My mother applied
VapoRub, set the humidifier
steaming, stroked my head
to reassure me things would be
alright. Doctors did me no good,
except to make me skeptical
of cures. Fighting for breath
bred in me a defensive posture.
Finally, my asthma just went
away, leaving me empathetic
to others' suffering — suffocated
by racism, poverty, abuse.
I am still waiting for the comfort
I was promised — the reassurance
that things will be set right.

Peg Leg Bates

Peg Leg Bates lost his leg
to a cotton gin when he was twelve.
I lost all trust from infancy—wondering
wordlessly when I would die. Peg Leg
loved to tap dance and got famous
for leaping five feet in the air to land
on his wooden leg. I got beaten first
then sexually abused landing
somewhere in nightmares later
because you don't forget that stuff.
Bates appeared on Ed Sullivan's
show twenty-one times, even
danced for the King of England.
All I want to do is entertain
myself with you. Mine is a dance
of a different kind. Sure, I don't
have a visible handicap.
You could call Peg Leg
a freak show but that would
be unkind. When he danced
it was graceful, remarkable.
You didn't feel his pain.
You didn't think of how they
cut off his mangled leg on his
mother's kitchen table.
Just let me dance—with you.
The abusers have left the room.

The Critical Weakness

I know it is a weakness to believe
everything one sees in dreams or reads
is true, but I do. I fall in love
with every heroine who asks
me to love her gently with slow
hands around her waist. I'm just
a sucker for a cheap romance.

Once, I listened as a student read
a story in my workshop. It must
have been a dream she'd had,
though she said fiction: She was
a teller in a bank, only there were
mirrors on every wall; the carpets,
furnishings, were fire-engine
red. A bandit entered, dressed
sleekly, all in black, demanded
that she take him to her vault.

And though she knew it was wrong,
she longed to lead him there, past
crystal chandeliers, mirrors reflecting
red around their faces. Only after he
had entered did she scream in fear.

I never told her that her dream was true;
only reassured her that some men
yearn equally for a gentle lover.

Gimme Culture

(The New York Times *reports average Americans will watch TV for nine years of their life.*)

After the third year the feeling
was mutual: we needed each other.
You setting quietly with a glow
on, me seated warm by your side.
I paid the bills, kept regular hours,
liked to see you turned on. You never
said you were addictive. Only,
after five years, you broke down.
"It was you that failed," I cried
into your unforgiving face. I pictured
you when you were young—
memories of a colorful reception,
your faded features bright again.
I got you fixed up and you seemed
to promise not to leave me. But even
a comfortable habit has to end.
Your funeral was rated fair for
the number of viewers and the early
hour it was on. I've tried it with others
since, but in their image I only see
the ghost of you. I'm dreadfully alone.

The Closest I've Come
To Being Normal

"Crap shoot. Life's a crap shoot."
Her soft eyes fix on me for sympathy.
"Once I wanted to be dead," she says.
"Tried to snuff myself." The pancake
makeup over what beard is left shows
the slight beads of sweat. Mascara
dilutes with tears. "How long did you
feel this way?" I ask in a voice
trained neutral by years of interviews.
"I've known I was different since
I was three. I suffered till twenty-seven."
Trans-sexual, a woman with balls, saving
for an operation. "The world is whacky,
anyway," I say, "Look at me." "Oh no,"
she reassures me, "I'm comfortable with you.
You're probably normal."

The Full Moon

The full moon maddens the blue jays
squawking good morning at one a.m.
If birds can be fools, what chance for me,
hot with hopes for a peaceful summer,
unable to dream or sleep? There, on the lawn
the largest grub I have ever seen,
its fat, white body fully fueled.
No one feeds more voraciously than I,
finding the secret insects burrowing
in my backyard, sucking them passionately.
Does a bird have a choice? Can nature
resist? This heat at last, ninety degrees in May
after so many cold nights, lusterless days.
Come on you crazy jays, scratch with me
in the moon-shadows of my back yard.
Let's devour these delicacies while we can.

A Guide To Suburban Birds

1. Parking-Lot Gulls
They preen beside puddles, squawking
over dumpster tidbits. Mother gull astride
a paper nest. Young gulls defending their
territory defined between white parking lines.
Old gulls like sailors too tired to go to sea.

2. Highway Hawks
The crows may leave the meadows
to pick at a recent roadkill.
Why should they bother with
field mice, harder now to find?
Here's fast food for any bird.
Only, a hundred feet above,
just at the edge of the pine barrens,
a hawk still spans the sky, waiting
for a movement he can identify.

3. Dump Swallows
Yes, gulls, circling noisily
above a dozer as it spreads their
dump-truck dinner. And yes, pigeons,
perhaps refugees from city streets,
cooing in a quieter corner. But also,
two swallows on a chain link, trying
to decide which home to buy.

Bird Understandings

Birds know how to die, anonymously,
only occasionally violating their code,
found mauled by the neighbor's
cat or crusted with gravel along
a road. We nearly never see them
perish, find no trace, though
thousands flock. They do not
trouble us for a funeral.

Imagine bird bone fields
where slight, white skeletons
bleach in beds of feathers,
a thousand wishbones awaiting
our hopeful tug. Or do they simply
fly so high they disappear?
Birds know death doesn't matter.

Misjudgments

The bird, hovering a moment,
slowing, misses its branch.
The squirrel who leaps from
its high perch, crash lands.
The raccoon miscalculates the car.
This is my natural state,
falling, crashing, crushed.
Yet, simply human, I lack
the dumbness of other animals,
with not so much as a mask
to cover my eyes.

The Buddhist Bird

From its unseen perch it calls to me,
"Right here. Right here." It's voice
is clear, it's message in the moment.

Bayberries are daily strewn across my
concrete walk. They are the elderly
surrendering to spring blossoms.

There it is, a cardinal, red plumage
as urgent as its call, "Right, right,
right here." We eye each other.

Today, the hickory tree has resurrected,
draping new leaves, just shy of flowers.
A neighbor told me it was dead.

I'm not one for bird calls, but I do my
best to answer, "Now, now, right now."
Cloudy-bright, moist air. Exquisite.

Torrey Pines, California

Atop Torrey Pines State Park
where the sun warms a spring
sea breeze, no one cares that
four phantom jets just turned
south toward factious Venezuela.
Surfers four hundred feet below
are idle dots, and hikers passing
prickly pears, chemise,
black sage, know only that
the beach trail is not just a walk
down, but back through fifty
million years of history—
strata of iron-rich sandstone,
fossil oyster shells—
so that for those emerging
from crevices carved
patiently by infrequent rains,
the passing fighters—high
as they fly, fast as they
disappear—are not half
so important as how
their sounds merge,
finally, with soft surf.

Spring The Age-Old Question

(For Adam & Eileen on their 25th anniversary.)

If pine weren't wisp,
linden a late spring
festival for noses;
if oak weren't a graduate
complete with tassel,
would we have hope?

If earth weren't a washer woman
with a sponge, the sky
a window cleaner,
would our lives be bright?

If zephyr weren't zither,
birds a reedy chorus,
the distant din of cars
a section of scratching strings,
could we know love?

Cold spring becomes
the sudden heat of summer.
Longer days remind us of
long nights we touched.

Campsite, Eraclea-Minoa, Sicily

The couple who played jumping
jack in the water, nude, both
giggling after, tangling waist-high
intimate at a farther extremity
of the beach; who kissed like Neptune
and his water nymph, writhing in brine;
walked proudly out of the water to eyes
aslant, glancing at them out of curiosity
or lust, sit dressed in dungarees now,
T-shirts loosely fit, not even leaning
close to talk over the supper table;
looking quite usual, but feeling
secretly naked.

Beach Countdown

Four boys with buckets
digging a sand foxhole,
a barricade for a war
the tide will win.

Three bathers wading
waist high in light chop—
hard to tell a he from a she,
so shallow so far out.

Two lovers on a Disney
towel, his hand on her
behind, her breasts
pressing on Goofy's face.

One patient fool,
back erect against
his beach chair,
ogling.

Weather Patterns

(For Nat and Nina Scammacca.)

With the subtlety of a pickpocket
a finger of cloud reaches for the sun,
a gold watch over the seasons.
One barely notices the cold sleight
of hand that follows,
so suddenly the summer
has been stolen.

November

November paints in grays,
midafternoon a patchwork
of low clouds silhouetting
leafless maples, filtering
the green from pitch pines.
Along the roadside, concrete
and stucco, house boards
even bricks turn gray,
as if fall has passed away
and November is in mourning.
A cold rush of air disappears
the last remaining oak leaves.

Midwinter, Stony Brook Harbor

The man in the Agway oil truck
parked by Stony Brook Harbor,
eats lunch, drinks an Orange Crush.
Fifty-two degrees at midday in February
on Long Island and the weatherman
promises more. The oilman tilts
his plastic bottle, one last swig,
but does not hurry, as if
to confirm that winter's over,
I'm-out-of-oil-burner-stopped
emergency calls are far behind.
Stretching elbows out
behind his head, bright sun
illuminates his face.
The tide rushes from wetlands
leaving mudflats oozing black —
surprisingly free of trash.
He reads his *Newsday*,
watches a moment more,
starts his route again.
Cold lingers in these waters
into July. Beyond his truck,
twelve or twenty boats,
cocooned in blue plastic or graying
canvas, await the subtle Sunday
afternoons of summer.

A Single Heron

There is a single heron,
tilts in the night waters
a foot poised
an eye for silver to flash
down—a patient fisher
after supper; teaches
me that balance counts
as much as speed, grace
an equal for any force.
From it I learn to swallow
life whole and down the gullet.

Autographs

The principle is called "contagious magic."
Someone or something has special powers.
You touch and the powers transfer to you.
It's worked since you caught that homerun
ball at the big league game and touched it
before you batted on the little league team.
The rabbit's foot—another story. Not
so lucky for the rabbit but an ancient sign—
where there were rabbits, with luck you,
too, could find lots of food. So, you stand
in line to get the autograph. Others may
see it as a quick way to make a buck
selling on eBay, but you know better.
If you get a NASCAR champ to sign, it
has to bring you better luck. Your car
will always start. You'll get to work on time.
If you get a picture of you two shaking hands,
frame the photo for your desk. "Is that you
with Earnhardt?" You'll get promoted,
a big raise and finally you can buy those
Daytona 500 Tower tickets that cost
a fortune but they come with the chance
to meet more drivers, get more autographs,
and like magic, you are sure to win.

Wishing

Wishing doesn't make it so
but it is such a lovely lie.
Every little symptom
reminds me that we all die.
The smallest cells that
gestate, in just a little while,
become the brain's blastoma
and our helpless, simian
smile. I wish I believed
in more than chance.

I have friends who insist
that prayer works. That's
as real for me as Hallmark
rhymes. What people wish
for does comes true sometimes.
That's called "coincidence."
Thinking there's more to life
than that is like believing
the world is flat. For me,
it's all just happenstance.

One For My Father

It was in a car he said he loved me,
plainly, for the first time, driving
with him from Long Island
to a second house I'd purchased
down in Florida. He had already
made clear that he objected:
"What do you need it for?" he asked.
"You'll never get your money back."
I couldn't tell him but I knew it was
another way to say, "Father, I am a person."
I tried to tell him, "I want to do something
for you." Of course, my offer to set him up
turned into his traveling to help me
fix the place. Of course, he told me he
didn't want me to: 1. make the property
a shelter to cut his taxes; 2. provide
a haven for his old age; 3. look after
him. But in between his bigshot son's
financial statements and his own meager
sense of what he needed, he reassured me
he did not want a fancy funeral, no year
of prayers, no Kaddish, no carrying on.
After all, he lived a simple life.
He was always sincere. And somewhere,
I think about Exit 3 on the New
Jersey Turnpike, he insisted that
he really loved me so I didn't have to
prove anything anymore.

The Last Time My Father Beat Me

The last time my father beat me
he was eighty-eight. He'd hit it
straight, one hundred twenty yards
to the green of his short course.
I'd spray one left or blow one well beyond.
His one sure putt, accomplished
without squatting to align. Once,
it was a chase into my bedroom where
he'd swing his leather belt. Now, he
smiled, squinting into the sunset.
Stiff as he was, I was never so
glad to see him swing that arm.

Honor Thy Father

My father made me go to Hebrew
school. Esoteric as it was to learn
an ancient language, when I was a kid
no one really spoke it—just old men
praying. Once a year, I was pushed
up front to shake my Zaydes' hands
and say, "L'shana tavah tikatevu."

Sit, stand, sit, stand, with sour-
mouthed people fasting. Nothing
sociable, mostly just my uncles
fund-raising for a new building.
When my last grandparent died,
my father admitted, "I did it all
for my father, but I don't believe."

"And, you," he told me, "don't
have to. Just do what you want."
By then, I was over thirty,
and though all my life I've heard
"Next year in Jerusalem," I don't
even care to go, though I still
light a *yahrzeit* for my father.

Curiosity

My mother liked to look in other people's
windows as she went walking. "Just
curiosity," she would say, "to get some
notion of how my rooms could look."
She'd put me in the stroller, or older,
I would march along with her,
stretching to see: a man in the kitchen
elbowing a metal table, his kids' toys
spread across the linoleum, supper
a greasy odor (not something to be seen).
But in richer neighborhoods (not ours),
she'd hesitate a step or stop—a slight hop
on one foot, higher, to see above the sill:
the Louis Quatorze loveseat, the couple
on their crushed-velvet couch, blanched
colorless by TV light, their beige wallpaper
printless in the shadows. Curiously,
as she got older (and so did I), my mother
still looked in windows and her house
was never redecorated in all those years.

Fingering

1.
My mother's fingers stiffened,
one by one, the knuckles
calcifying until none could bend.
No more easy grasp at clasps
of teal costume jewelry she
loved to ornament her velvet
blouse. No more curled caress
of the piano keys or light touch
of pastels to bring portraits to life.
The only certainty—her wedding ring
would not come off until her death.

2.
My friend's fingers are locked
in arcs, awkwardly pointing in
or out. Can they find right letters
on her ergonomic keyboard she
purchased because of repetitive
stress, her wrists also wearing
out? To use her pen is more
choreography than flex, her whole
hand moving to form the shapes.
There's "speak and type," so
the ideas may still come out.

3.

"Ossification: hardening (as in
muscular tissue) into a bony
substance." I bend my fingers
around as tightly as I can
despite the pain. This cessation
won't occur without a fight.
Slow rigor mortis, genetic
clock pointing toward a late-
round loss. I open and close
my fist, examining the knuckles,
not yet ready to capitulate.

Celebrate Good Times

Why my mother didn't like
celebrations is complicated.
No holiday was sacred. Beyond
an ethnic antipathy to Christmas,
she joked that Jewish Valentines
Day was February 15, when the candy
was half priced, laughing equally at
cheap-Jew stereotypes and "all that
sentimental tripe." For her wedding,
she and my dad eloped—a simple justice
of the peace—forever infuriating her
Orthodox in-laws. Even for her fiftieth
anniversary, barely a mention—though
her marriage was sound. For ninety-one
years, her birthdays weren't important.
Was it child-of-the-Depression frugality?
She squeezed a nickel until the buffalo
choked—but, actually, was very generous.
Perhaps, she thought herself unworthy.
Though she painted portraits better
than some famous artists, she never
advertised her talents. Self effacing?
A little, but most of all she told me
that, deep in her atheist heart,
she knew, "Life is no big deal.
Live it and be done." Who are we
to celebrate, as if we are a gift
in some God's creation?

Seder In The Jewish Nursing Home

Why Passover? We want you angel
to stop this very night for mercy
do not forsake those in nursing homes
first born or not, take them.
We are waiting for you, old dependable,
doer of God's work, to set us free
of choking fits and catheters,
of recalcitrant attendants, of waiting
every day for you. So don't pass over,
rather come quickly, as we've
let the lambs live and scrubbed
the doors to our rooms and will laugh
at your countenance and welcome
you even as you prey. We pray
for you let our people go.

Caution: Cancer Causes Poetry

So many people—academics,
probation officers, cab drivers,
waitresses—all writing poetry,
lamenting lost breasts; glad
to be rid of festering colons
despite the colostomy bags.
Holding notebooks, iPads,
waiting for open mics,
proclaiming remission.
Or, confessing metastases,
consoling themselves they
fought it the best way they could.
But wait, now you think I am
unsympathetic. You are mistaken.
I am the one who advocates
the healing power of poetry,
encourages first chapbooks,
believes even beginners should
be taken seriously. But, for all
the lines written on order forms,
hotel notepads, tiny qwerty
keyboards, I'm tired of how
cancer causes poetry when
we need much more than
empathy. We need a cure.

½ Scientist, ½ Woman

The breast came back to
question her on weekends
as if asking for a date,
demanding what could have
caused her to grow so
strange. "A cancer," was
the only answer she could
muster, "and I'm glad you're
gone!" But lying pillowed,
late and dark, as other parts
debated their revolt, she felt
a hollowness around her heart
and wondered if the breast
might not be right. Better
stay whole than slowly dragged
apart. When several organs
celebrated their independence
with a fireworks of tissues,
she solemnly declared and
issued "No further surgery."
Subsequently, she remarried
to the breast in a quiet
ceremony. (The specialist
insisted that he might
have saved her.)

Curing Rilke

("If my devils leave me, I'm afraid my angels
will take flight as well.")

So said Rainer Maria Rilke,
but he was haunted by disembodied
hands and I often dwell in fantasy.
Was it Byron who said he saw
the ghosts of impending imbecility?
Now, we live long enough to fear
forgetting "me." And there's no cure
beyond stupefying pills forced on
the senile and elderly. For trauma,
perhaps there's therapy: a short
interview, a trusting induction,
and poof—release, but leaving what?
An infant's early yearnings? A scholar's
tabula rasa? I shall dwell in these
dark, familiar thoughts until there is
nothing left of me. If my devils
leave me, will my angels also flee?

The Savior

You ask me, "If the house
were burning, what would
you save?" Would it be
my photo albums? Odd how
printing pictures has all but
stopped. I don't own jewelry,
though I imagine gold melting
to nuggets in someone else's fire.
The cat can save itself with
a leap when the door is opened.
I'd see to that, and my wife
is similarly fleet of foot. Yes,
I'd shoo them out. Important
papers? I'd want my kids to
have my will—odd word,
with many meanings, first
asking what we want to do
with life, then how to dispose
of it. My safe, I'm told, is
fireproof to fifteen hundred
Fahrenheit, which will cremate
me, should I linger to breathe
in smoke and choke. Lately,
I wonder if I'd save myself.

The Dirty Old Man

Left alone by the death
of a spouse, a dirty old
man needs love. Long
in the fang but short on
stamina, stirred by an
ancient lust, he watches
young women passing by.
An old man, bald, bearded,
who has bought a fast car,
dressed in his Bill Blass
blazer, ventures into
a bar, his pocket filled
with cash. There are women
less than half his age who
let him buy them drinks.
One tells him tales of abuse.
"Daddy beat me and so did
my ex." An old man takes her
home, lets her use the bathroom,
waits in his boxer shorts on
the edge of the bed. Next
morning, after he's scrambled
her eggs topped with Velveeta,
she promises they can meet
at the same bar, soon, but
doesn't set a time. There

are polite goodbyes and her
exit. Reaching for the Old Spice,
an old man notices missing
bottles of his dead wife's last
painkillers kept in the medicine
cabinet in case his own life
isn't worth living anymore.

Alone In Your House

I open drawers like Hawkshaw
the Detective, careful
not to leave a clue that I've
been there, searching for who
you really are: I note the tranquilizers
in your medicine chest, the hair
dye for your wife, a pint of Kaopectate.
But in the bureau you give yourselves
away, not in the bank book tucked in
the back (four hundred sixty dollars
left of all you've ever earned) but
in the diary your wife has hidden in
her underwear, the days checked off
infrequently when you have been
successful; and in the nightstand
drawer, left beneath the gap-toothed
comb and dirty tissues, a dozen
prophylactics safe in their hygienic
seals. I close the door on the same
tragedies I know, sorry to see you
like myself—promise to say something
erotic to your wife to turn her
on for you when you two return.

Clorox Clean

The most effective mix is
ten to one to kill whatever germs.
Overdosing, I pour it straight from
the bottle to the floor. I don't wear
clothes I value. Alone, I might
wear only underwear, spreading
the liquid with a rag as my eyes
tear. I've burned off my fingerprints,
bleached my knees and soles.
Lungs scorched, I cough as I
cry for all my blemishes.

From Such Meditations

(A Chi Gong exercise.)

In the meditation room the scent
of sandalwood is strong. Remove
glasses, rings, shoes, settle into
a stance—feet shoulders wide,
knees slightly bent. Eyes closed,
let your thoughts glide from
a talking head to a more silent
center. Breathe deeply, slowly,
shoulders drooping. Thoughts
become less specific, going
from "Here I am, looking how?"
to just being there without others.
Now, move something but only
if something moves you. Lean
to the side, or rock back and
forth, sensing the quality of light,
texture of air, a slight vibration
as you bring your cupped hands
up waist-high in front of you.
Breathe good energy in. Let dark
energy out. Bring comfort up
from the giving earth. Let sad
energy drain to the accepting earth.
Remain in place until you feel
satisfied. Be glad you are alive.

Meditation On My 1979 MGB

More than an object, it is
a way of life—observing each
part, cataloging it: the crumbling
windshield gasket and the worn
window fuzzies; the lovely, new
electronic choke and aluminum
header. What is old can be fixed,
polished or, as often, replaced.
Even the lights that illuminated
its early owners now can shine
anew. Where there is rust, one
can weld. For a dent, a ball-peen
hammer and Bondo. More than
a hobby, this is a resurrection.

The Snowbird's Sonnet

The promise of an endless summer brought
me here. Daytona Beach, with hard, flat sand,
green surf, an amphitheater where a band
performs for free on summer nights. I thought
the warmth of Florida would compensate
for all the ice and snow I had to clear—
an end to winter doldrums and the fear
I'd never leave that endless, frozen state.
I hadn't calculated how far north
I picked, or how one summer thins the blood,
so nights in forties, days just sixty would
require a jacket when I venture forth.
It isn't freezing. Sure, I'm glad for that.
I wear a bathing suit and woolen hat.

Sun Worship

The dermatologist burns a dozen spots
off me with liquid nitrogen. For all I
know, at sixty bucks a pop, he could just be
making this up to pay for his Mercedes.
He tells me the sun is dangerous — wear
a hat, use tons of sunscreen. I'm stupid.
I still love the sun, luxuriating in my
backyard with a book and iced tea.
They tell me it's a hole in the ozone
or maybe a solar eruption that sends
radiation straight at me. Basal cell
this and squamous that and oh,
the dreaded melanoma. Perspiration
streams down my solar plexus. I'm
oiled and browned. No one can
tell me Vitamin D stands for death.

Florida Haikus And Tankas

Resurrection fern
curled closed and brown, opens green
with just a little rain.

Hibiscus blossoms—
look like crepe-paper flowers—
touched, moist, supple, soft.

Palm trees grow old with
pride, their rings outside. Oak trees
show age post mortem.

Schizophrenic days—
pouring on one street corner,
sun on the other.

Complain lawn sprinklers
smell like sulfur water or
see rainbows in mist.

Key West deer among
bent pines of Boca Chica
stay small to survive.

A philodendron
leaves its pot to dominate
buttressed banyan trees.

Little old lady
by concrete bench, Ocean Ave.,

her three-wheel walker
V-handlebars with bike brakes,
her hands high, still holding on.

Gangly old jogger
hands dangling hip high, hardly
faster than a walk.

Grandma paddling, gray
one-piece and rubber flowered
cap, grandkids splashing.

Old man has a hitch
in his giddy up. Dipping
his left hip, he walks
briskly, nonetheless. Eighty,
he's recovered from the stroke.

He's three hundred pounds
trying to catch a Frisbee.
She's done up in string
bikini, coconut oiled,
ready to catch guys who eye her.

She's four. Daddy's
caught a hermit crab that pokes
a tentative claw.
She smacks it with a shovel
but the crab knows what to do.

Leaning on car hood
hollering into cell phone—
startling white surf,

a mile of sand, brilliant blue
sky—she argues with some guy.

Boy on boogie board
gravity, liquidity
speeding along waves.

She's playing catch-up,
piling buckets of sand where
waves strike her castle.

Two men on a dock
with a dozen snappers—catch
of the day—smiling.

Ten gray pelicans
glide a straight line south along
dunes and A1A.

92 at dusk
motor scooter heading home
simmers evening sounds.

In Favor Of A New Poet Laureate

(Read into the record on the floor of Florida State Senate by Senator Dorothy Hukill on the occasion of creating a four-year, renewable post of Florida Poet Laureate. April 23, 2014.)

We need poems the way we
need rainbows. It's not like we
believe in the pot of gold, but
beauty is a thing to behold,
and a little fantasy can be fun.
It's time for the Legislature
to get the task done. Pass this
bill for all the talented writers
who promote literacy and
delight us with their poems.
The legislation won't cost
the State a dime, as surely
as poems don't always have
to rhyme. Sometimes, they just
paint beautiful pictures.

The End Of The Universe

A boy with a glandular disorder grows taller than God. "You've done it now," he shouts at the Deity, gazing down at God's balding head. "A mere boy and I'm already taller than my Father." "Why do children always expect perfection from their parents?" God laments. "You made me, didn't you?" the boy insists. "You're a big boy, now," God says, "Fix yourself." "If I could do that," the boy cries, "I would be like God, knowing the secrets of life and death." "Yes, of course, we couldn't have that, could we?" says God. "I don't imagine you'd consider just kneeling before me so you'd appear shorter?" "Not on your life," says the boy. "It's bad enough to grow up and see the defects of one's parents; it's another thing to grovel and kneel. Besides," the boy points out, "I'm still growing. I'm so tall, now, if I kneeled I'd look you in the eye and that's not decent. You are the Deity, after all." "I'm glad you still know your place," God says. "And what is that?" the boy inquires. "A mere speck in our vast universe," God replies. "Well," says the boy, "You'd better expand the universe because my head just bumped the end of it."

The Man Who Fell In Love With His Chicken

(For Russell Edson.)

A man and a chicken were in love. The man said, "I love you, Chicken. I love your spindly legs, your feathered ass, your hard lips." The chicken could tell false flattery. She wasn't going to be had. "Pluck," she said. "Chicken," the man said, "why do you withhold your charms? Take me in your arms. I do love you. You know I do, for my heart is light as a feather and it sings." "Pluck, pluck," the chicken said batting her wings, and "pluck" again for emphasis. But now the man was angry. "You plucking chicken," he said, "I know the truth about you and so will the world. The egg came first. You aren't the pure young thing you play at. You've been laid before." The chicken paled with fright. All night feathers flew. She grew old before her time and bald, plucked from her youth untimely. And the man, seeing her so naked and frail, reaffirmed his love and ate her.

A Lesson In Friendship

A lonely man leaves his window open and his light on. Soon, his room is filled with moths—hairy brown, delicate white, tints of tan and yellow. "Now I have friends," he says, "even if they are only the souls of the dead passing on to heaven or hell." He deals a hand of gin, pours drinks, serves pretzels. Aside from their dust, he finds them agreeable. "I hope you don't think of his as purgatory," he says. "No, not at all," a Virgin Tiger Moth replies, "I think of this as a last fling before the flame." "Excuse me," the man informs his mothy friends, "I must go potty." But when he returns he catches an Eight-spotted Forester peeking at the cards. "Really," the man shouts, "If you are going to be my friends, couldn't you at least try to transcend the caterpillar?"

Tongue Hotel

(For Emily.)

Pancake, don't cry. Come into this fine mouth hotel with carpet tongue and gum-ridged bar with ivory teeth for seats and warm pools for you to soak your feet. Pancake, don't fear that tunnel you face, winding down to darker places. Once you were a whole big piece, but someone has cut you into littler pieces. I've poured this syrup over you to ease the pain. Don't you wish you were whole again? Follow my tongue, I tell you. There is where to enter. Your family is waiting.

For The Birds

1.
Something about birds
makes them disagree.
Perhaps it's their feathers —
too many kinds and colors.
See birds sorted out in oaks
by species, as if bird feces
aren't all equal. It doesn't
matter if it's a willow or
a teak, birds find a way
to disagree. That's how
hawks make all their money.

2.
Always there are wars
where birds are enemies
or brothers — a pecking
order for bird strangers
and lovers, beaks for
grooming, and beaks
for dooming. Clearly,
humans are much better —
our history proving
how peacefully we
live together.

3.

Oh, not so, you say?
Well, we would be
fine and peaceful
people, not inflicting
pain and preaching
war beneath each
dome and steeple,
except humans are
bereft of reason when
it is political season, using
only their bird brains.

Animal Truths

Dogs don't dissemble.
For a biscuit, they roll
over and tell the truth.
Even sleeping on
a couch, their legs
run romps for rabbits.
Cats need deeper
analysis. They're further
along in perfidy,
sneaky eyes
mousing around,
always indirect.
Don't believe canaries.
They can't be trusted,
tweeting wildly
but dead before
their testimony
can be sworn.

Cockroach Immortality

I joke I've taught the bigger ones
to sing, or saddled them to ride,
but like B-movie scenes where
hoards are revealed, finding even
one in a corner is a bad dream.
I've seen them frolic on sidewalks
at night, provoking screams.
"It's just a palmetto bug," a pretty
euphemism we tell tourists. I buy
a contract to protect my house.
"To heck with the EPA; spray
everywhere." But there they are,
belly-up in corners, their crooked
legs still kicking. Are there cockroach
EMTs, little medics waiting
to rescue them with cockroach CPR?
I reach for them with paper towels.
The less dead roll over and make a run.
Later, a dry carcass greets me like
a taxidermy trophy. Three hundred
million years they've practiced.
Humans have been here merely thirty
thousand years. Four thousand species
inhabit what we call our world. I have,
perhaps twenty years before I'm gone.
Their kind will have three hundred
million more. What makes me
think that I can win this war?

The Myth Of Mathematics

As if we need even basic
computation now that every-
one has calculators. Writing,
speaking—computers can't
argue a point or create. We live
well without algebra, consume
without calculus, use our GPS
without geometry. Life without
language facility—handicapped.
Take the SATs, the GREs and
write a killer essay, it's not
taken seriously. But if you
get low math scores, they
turn you away. What's needed
to do some things is clear,
as with professional athletes:
in basketball, shoot 75% from
the foul line; for baseball, hit 250.
You can't deny the need for hand-
eye coordination. But what's with
the myth of math? What we
need is more poetry and music—
or are we only calculating
the trajectory of weapons?

Soccer

What genius invented soccer?
Hefty calves plying muddy fields.
Any sport requiring the head
to stop hard flying objects—duh!
And who is the fool screaming,
"Goal! Goal! Goal!" Imagine
a couple hours and a 1-1 tie?
Duh times two.
     We're stuck
with baseball, the boring boys
of summer. We're hooked
on basketball, a hyper-
glandular parade. Wrestling?
Stupidity. Hockey? Stupidity on ice.
Football? Steroids in uniform.
But soccer? Exceptionally dumb!

Hoop Dreams

Why I thought I could make it
could be explained in therapy,
but the easy answer was that
at thirteen a kid has a right
to dream. Dressed in khaki gym
shorts and high-top sneakers,
I dribbled down the court, broke
right and leaped for a layup.
The ball ricocheted nowhere near
the net. Why the coach made me
guard the biggest kid I can't say.
I bounced off him as he ran
down-court, and I was called
for the foul. Later, I tossed one
up from nearly half-court,
imagined the silence as a hopeful
crowd waited for me to win
the game. The ball rolled round
and round the rim and didn't
fall in. I persisted through
however many practices,
showed up on Saturday for
a bus to take us to a crosstown
rival. "Didn't you read the list?"
the coach chided as the doors
closed and the team pulled away.

Little League

Little League was never far
in spring, only we weren't just
trying out, we were reporting.
Maybe not Winter Haven
or Sarasota, but we saw the pros
beside us who could win one
in the clutch, save one with a leap,
homer into the upper deck. But we
would show them. One winter
dreaming could shape a kid into
a star. Last season's fatal strikeout—
a game transforming double;
the missed hard grounder—
a quick turn around the horn
retiring the side. The coach
steps up to an ungroomed plate,
tosses high the first white ball
for fielding and crack, it's coming
at you. Spring! Spring at last toward
your chance to make the team. Except
for that one wet spot along the baseline—
the slip, the fall. And then the long
walk home, slapping the mud from
your dungarees, swearing,
"Next time, next time," the newness
of the season already gone.

Dry-Mouth Syndrome

("I spit on you. You spit on me. In this we have equality."
—John Childs)

The fellow who owned
property across from me
pounded his fist into his
hand chanting, "Jew, Jew,"
and told me, "Hitler
didn't do the job well enough,"
and, "We have lampshades
made from people like you,"
so I called him a Nazi.
Later, the Human Rights
Commission said, "You
made it a spitting contest
when you insulted him."
They would not file my
formal complaint. I am
found guilty of being Spittish.

Forgive And Forget

I think there is enough forgiveness
in the world that I don't need to,
let alone forget. Someone must
decry the villainy; someone must
scream at the blows others strike
on the backs of children,
on the cheeks of wives,
on the knuckles held out to nuns,
the feet bastinadoed, the bellies
of unwanted pregnancies.
Someone should hold accountable
mass murderers who cannot
just be absolved by a confession.
I'll take the job, though not willingly.
I might as well—I who have witnessed
and endured abuse; I who sit
weeping at the nightly news.

The South Still Rises

Driving Interstate I-4 I see it
flying from a tall, steel pole—
a 30′ x 50′ Confederate flag
raised by the Sons of the Confederacy.
And there it is again, on I-75
as I get off to see the Cultural
Center on the Suwannee River
that features dioramas of Stephen
Foster's happy slaves. In Tallahassee,
the Capitol displays Dixie
flags for Confederate Memorial
Day. The State of Georgia fought
long and hard to keep the Stars
and Bars on its State flag.
At Stone Mountain—where
Confederate generals are
carved in granite—they still
wave the flag, sing Dixie
and hope the South will rise
again. Lecture me again on
free speech. That flag is hate
speech that honors slavery.

Shooting Doves

("On the wings of a snow white dove, he sends his pure, sweet love. A sign from above, on the wings of a dove." Sung by Ferlin Husky.)

"On the wings of a snow white dove."
That's all I could hear in my head
after I hung up. My son told me
he took a flying lesson. "You did well,"
his instructor said, "you even made
a 360° turn. Most first fliers
get scared. You were cool up there."
But it was what my son said next
that threw me.

On the wings of a snow white dove ...

My son is loud, has my inappropriate
sense of humor, makes some people
nervous, but he has a serious side.
"While I was flying," he told me,
"I wasn't scared. I just kept telling
myself, 'I've lived a full life. If I crash,
I may be frightened falling, but then

there'd be no pain.'" My words and I
don't even remember saying them to him.

On the wings of a snow white dove ...

I wish I had other people's faith. As if He
sends His love—with all the suffering and
murders. My own mother, who watched
the Holocaust, said, "If there's a God
he must be a bastard." As if I believe
in a God or a Goddess, or any sign
from above on the wings of a dove.

They say there are no atheists when
there's turbulence on an airplane.
Let others pray. Me, I'm smiling
because it will be the end of pain.
You see, I don't think of "snow"
or "white" or "doves." Maybe,
I see vultures waiting to pick
my bones—an air funeral where
Buddhist monks cut me into chunks
and leave me for the birds to carry off.
So you can keep your wings of
snow white doves.

Nothing swoops down to save you.
No ever-lasting love—just an end

to a world of sarin gas and gunfire,
robberies and virulent prejudice.
All the Gospels in the world can't
save me, and now my son has learned
my song—and it's not Ferlin Husky,
or even Elvis Presley singing corny
lyrics to a teary crowd. It isn't even
atheism, which I think is just another
sad religion.

On the wings of a snow white dove ...

I see the sweet lies they feed us from above,
offering salvation in another world instead
of relief from our present greed and pain.
Let my son and me and anyone who is brave
soar on our own—with no fear of hell or
consequences—just living life with a hope
that in one quick fall we will be blessed
with an end to all this hypocrisy and strife.

Cop Story

I've been driving on the highway
for about twelve hours but when
I get off, it's too soon. My motel
is on the east side of the city, and
I've exited on the west. It's midnight
on a cold, rainy night, and I find
a wide boulevard that runs
crosstown. I'm not thinking
about my speed until I see
the flashing lights of the cop car
behind me, pulling me over.
I figure maybe I can save the cop
some trouble if I get out of my car
and walk over to him. Maybe,
I can talk my way out of the ticket.
But as I approach, he jumps out
of the car and hollers, "What
are you doing? Get back in
the car. I want your license
and registration." I walk
to the rear of my car to open
my trunk. I've got my briefcase
in it and I need to retrieve
the information. As the trunk
lid pops open and I reach down
to get what I need, I hear him shout
something. I turn with my briefcase
in my hand to find him standing
in full firing position—feet spread,
hands stretched out toward me with his

gun aimed straight at me. "I said 'freeze,'"
he shouts at me. "What are you doing?"
"I had to get my license out," I tell him.
"Put the briefcase on the ground,"
he orders me, adding, "slowly."
I do, and he tells me to, "Take
the license out, slowly."
I do, and he tells me, "Get back
in your car and wait for me,"
just beginning to lower the gun.
I scurry into the car with my wallet
and briefcase. He follows me to my
window and takes my papers back
to the cop car. I wait awhile until he
returns to hand my papers back together
with a speeding ticket. As I watch him
drive away, I think to myself, "If I were
Black, I would be dead. He wouldn't
have waited to see what I was doing
when I turned. I'd be lying in the gutter
with however many bullets in me.
He gave me the benefit of the doubt."
I can't help thinking, "It's America.
It shouldn't be this way, but life is
dangerous—much more dangerous
for some people than others."
I can't help but ask myself,
"Should I be grateful that I'm
White or feel guilty?"

Heritage

Tovarishch Stalin byl tverdyy paren'.
Stalin byl tiranom.
Stalin sdelal yego narod sil'nym.
Stalin byl zlodeyem.
Eto vse v glazakh smotryashchego.
Zhalost' umer tak mnogo lyudey.

Comrade Stalin was a solid guy.
Stalin was a tyrant.
Stalin made his nation strong.
Stalin was a villain.
It's all in the eye of the beholder.
Pity so many people died.

Hitler war ein schöner Mann.
Hitler war der Teufel.
Hitler gekämpft, um sein Land zu retten.
„Heil Hitler!" sollte illegal sein.
Es ist alles, wie Sie es sehen.
Schade um den Holocaust.

Hitler was a handsome man.
Hitler was the devil.
Hitler fought to save our land.
"Heil Hitler!" should be

illegal. It's just how you see it.
Pity about the Holocaust.

The Confederate flag is my heritage.
The Confederate flag stands for treason.
The Confederate flag, long may it fly.
Take it down for a good reason.
It's just how you see it.
Pity about racial hatred.

Prejudice

Prejudice is a great fault
of the mind and though I am
sometimes smart, I simply
can't understand it, except
it is a close cousin to injustice,
which considers not facts but
stupid statements like, "You're
all a pack of lazy criminals
so you must be guilty."
I, myself, am guilty of ducking
injustice. I've done nothing
about those profitable prisons
the people in power have built.
But I work at not being fooled,
and perhaps, if I simply speak
often and loudly, I can help—
or maybe I need to get a big
F-ing sledge hammer and
tear those buildings down.

Guilty

A salt mist rises along the shore.
A steady wind renders sunrise
cool to the skin despite the warmth
of summer. Who first noticed
the horizon curves or mused that
the sun does not sizzle rising
from the sea? We live in this
fortunate land where others lived
long before us. As far down
the beach as we can see were
tribes we met and murdered,
then scraped from the curve
of memory. Oceans matter,
lasting longer than aristocracy.
Salt pounds to vapor, rising
in the swells to break on the beach.
What we have now was stolen.
Shouldn't we, witness to such
beauty, feel guilty?

Black Friends

"Black Friends" should not
be the title of this but it has to be
because I don't see any Black
families owning houses in my
neighborhood so when I have
friends come visit—who stay
with me—first, I have to tell
my lovely White neighbor
next door, "I have a professor
friend coming to stay, so if you
see a Black man walking between
our houses, please don't get
nervous and call the cops,"
and she demures, "Oh,
you don't have to worry," then
pauses, adding "but thanks for
telling me." Except, when another
Black friend—a psychologist
(not that it matters what he does,
but I feel compelled to qualify that
these friends aren't the ordinary,
working people I know who
sometimes stop by in their
broken-down pickup truck, all
sweaty and the same neighbor
asked me, "Who were those scary
people parked in front of your
house?")—when my clinical
psychologist friend quietly left
my house his first morning to

see the sunrise, someone at the end
of my street I don't know by name
but I often wave to, coming out of his
house to get the morning paper,
told my friend when he asked,
"I turn this way to get to the ocean?"
told him, "No, the water is that way,"
and turned my friend away toward
the road out of our neighborhood,
convincing me that it is true: no
Black families are being shown
houses for sale in my "area," which
I no longer really think of as "my
neighborhood" because I am so ashamed.

Homeless

Standing in the narrow traffic island,
she holds no sign but is clearly
begging. It is brutally hot, cars
queued up, windows closed for a/c.
Her lips purse but she says nothing
as she draws her shoulders up
as if to duck, grasps the bottom
edge of her tattered tee-shirt
and stretches it to wipe her brow
revealing a too-skinny midriff.
Her eyes squint into the sun.
Her knees bend and unbend,
close to collapse, yet she persists,
holding out a hand toward traffic,
shrugging to mop her brow,
cringing as motors rev each change
of the light. A window opens
half way, and she moves closer.
"Get a job," a young man shouts.

On Being Safe

His mantra starts out,
"Warm, clean, comfortable."
He's had his share of troubles —
health, work, relationships.
He's never been consoled to hear
others have it so much worse.
Why would that make him feel
better? How many people go hungry,
combing dumpsters for food,
or sleep in cardboard boxes
in freezing weather? Others
may see him as a "kook." At least
he's not a criminal, eyeing what
others have, ready to pounce.
Nor is he filled with ethnic hatred.
In the darkness of his bedroom,
a cover pulled over his ear,
for a moment he's grateful
he is not in danger and he
can safely fall asleep.

Calling Out Their Names

Amadou Diallo, Trayvon Martin,
Jose Guerena, Eleanor Bumpurs,
Tamir Rice, Michael Brown,
Freddie Gray, Oscar Grant III,
Kenneth Chamberlain, Fong Lee.
You can't make a full list —
it's too long. The ones they beat
nearly to death, the ones they murdered.
We cry for the dead, but what
about the living: My activist friend,
Marvin, who's been arrested ten
times at peaceful protests. Donald,
who marched against the war,
was arrested and jailed just one
night at Riker's Island. Raped,
he contracted AIDS and died —
the death penalty for his free
speech. My Black colleague,
a professor who has owned
a home in his small college town
for over twenty years but still
gets stopped by the cops on
evenings when he takes a walk:
"Can we see some ID, sir?"
He even knows their names.
"It's me, Sam," he tells them.
"Just some ID," they intone
and he knows if he resists at all
he'll be in danger. That list is
longer than most of our lives,

dates back to animals fighting
for territory long before there
were even people. What part
of our DNA makes us attack?
How long before we can find
our better nature?

The Suffering Goes Both Ways

(A "Swastika Poem" for William Heyen.)

The German-American boy of six,
what could he understand of war or pain?
His father, scraped the swastikas off
where they'd been smeared on the front door.
The boy was only six. His immigrant father
worked in a defense plant on Long Island
riveting the fuselage of Douglas DC3s.
What could a boy know of Bergen-Belsen,
Buchenwald? When the news came that
Roosevelt was dead, the boy cried because
he couldn't go to the picture show his mother
promised. But Hitler, hidden deep within
the bunkers beneath Berlin, stamped
and screamed the Gods had sent a sign
his Reich would rise again from ashes
and bombed-out cities.

When the boy was twenty-three he visited
Germany and the family who'd stayed
behind. One older aunt served tea and
strudel which he savored, but he had
to ask her, what was she doing during
the war? How could it have happened?
It was then she dropped the smile,
the fond expression for this brother's
son, and in a voice like testimony
at a trial, she explained:

Your Uncle Max and I, we had
our camera store. He was alive then.
We had a family and our business.
So, I would walk from work, past the train
tracks and the depot, and I would hear
some voices moaning, and once I think I saw
a hand sticking out of a boxcar.
But it was the war. That wasn't
anybody's business. What could I
do? Only once ... once I was walking
home and the smoke—you know,
the smoke—I smelled it and I shouldn't
say this. It was late, supper time
you know, and I couldn't help myself
from thinking it smelled
like pot roast cooking.

So very human her response,
he finally understood.

Short Course On
The Holocaust

You see, my dear readers, I hesitate
to write this down and will
only do it if you promise to believe me.
I was performing poems until late
one winter afternoon, in the Egyptian
Room of the Brooklyn Museum, and when
I finished a woman I'd been warned of
greeted me with a banal rhyme about poetry
itself and thanked me cockeyed for my
reading. All the while she talked, we stood
before the massive sarcophagus of an ancient
Pharaoh. Behind it, because it was sunset,
a Hasidic Jew stood davening facing
the wall, bent and unbent in prayer,
his black hat bobbing, his peyas
curled to his cheeks. Believe me,
life itself is strange, and we are
always in danger. It's a wonder
with all this madness
who survives!

All Vows

(Kol Nidre.)

All vows that you forced from me,
my chest pressed to the concrete,
my haunches raised toward you
in supplication — all those promises —
I renounce. To be brothers,
to be friends, to be forgiving,
to set aside all anger and pretend
that life is better than before,
all such vows I cancel now.
No testimony given under torture
is true. No apology will suffice
from you. All vows I have made —
that you should suffer, that you
should pay, that you should be brought
as low as you brought me — all those
plans I have made that pretend justice,
I abandon now. It is time, though my
gut burns with the acid of your insults,
and I am addicted to the pain. Today,
I cancel all consecrations; I spit on
what you say is sacred. It is a new
year and it is time to renounce all vows.

Once In A While A Protest Poem

Over and over again the papers print
the dried out tit of an African woman
holding her starving child. Over
and over, cropping it each time to one
prominent, withered tit, the feeble
infant face. Over and over to toughen
us, teach us to ignore the foam turned
dusty powder on the infant's lips,
the mother's sunken face (is cropped)
and filthy dress. The tit remains;
the tit held out for everyone to see,
reminding us only that we are not so hungry
ogling the tit, admiring it and in our
living rooms, making it a symbol of starving
millions; our sympathy as real as silicone.

Why I Cut My Barber

I've been going to a father
and son shop where it's been clear
the eighty-six-year-old dad doesn't
see too well, so I sit down for his
errant son who dad once told me,
"shows up late but does know how
to cut good." As sonny starts, he
asks me, "What do you think of
those Dumocrats? They're ruining
America." Dummy that I am, I tell
a man holding a sharp object next
to me, "OMG, are you really going
there? Get over it." He quickly
concludes the haircut—barely
having done a thing. I pay him
his ten bucks but swear he's too
dangerous for me to go back again.

Mandatory Reporting

They move in the shadows
Where no one can see
And they're chainin' up people
And they're bringin' 'em to me
Askin' me, "Kill them now, or later?"
So sings Brecht's Pirate Jenny.

If it were up to me and the Pirate Jenny,
all the bastards would be executed.
That would leave a few friends
and me to clean up and get on
with the job of living. After all,
it's just a game—ego and fame—
as if anyone lives forever. You can work
all your life, please the boss and your wife,
but the end is the same for every sailor.

Poets who tinker, politicians and stinkers,
priests, police and jailors, the end
is the same for every sailor.

I've worked very hard, learned a lot
that I forgot, or worse, there's too much
I remember. To discuss one's plans
may win you some fans but too often
it's to confess your failings. For full forty years,
I've sought out your cheers

and I think that I have earned them. Then,
some stranger or fool breaks all the rules,
and in the end it's the same for every sailor.

Poets who tinker, politicians and stinkers,
priests, police and jailors, the end
is the same for every sailor.

Ask what it's all about and I'll leave you
in doubt. It's better to not be specific.
Some people love their wine, live their lives
quite refined. Some say I'm the king of
the whiners. I'll just take it and smile.
You don't hear me complain.
(Okay, here comes the refrain.)
Life isn't logical or fair. In the end
it's the same for every sailor.

Poets who tinker, politicians and stinkers,
priests, police and jailors, the end
is the same for every sailor.

And in that quiet of death I'll say
"Right now. Right now!"
Then they pile up the bodies
And I'll say, "That'll learn ya!"
Or, so says the Pirate Jenny.

Surprises

(With thanks to Dr. Marvin Levine.)

For some, there are no surprises.
Their Goddess watches over them
while others prefer a bearded old
man and think everything is pre-
destined. If the Reaper opens my door
and gestures toward me, I'll laugh.
"What are you laughing at, you
damned fool?" Death will say,
"I'm here for your soul."
"Given a lifetime of doubt, if
you are real, think of all the other
possibilities," says me.
"You aren't listening," he or
she might say, "It's the big one
and hey, maybe even hell."
But I've been married twice
before—which may explain my
lack of faith—and both ex-
wives told me to go to hell.
For me, life is full of surprises.

The Dead Have No Respect

When she died he had her decked
out better than she'd looked in life,
only to have her run away with
some sailor they called Charon.

Contact Myth

Once there was a girl who loved
rubbing: forehead on cold windows,
fingers through shag rugs, feet
across hot sand, tongue over salty
pretzel's crystals. She wanted contact,
rubbing her cheeks on velvet pillows
and, when no one looked, she leaned
to press them on bold Formica table-
tops. As she grew, she rubbed her knees
against the legs of tables, her bottom,
bare, against hard, slippery chairs,
and once herself against the bathtub.
She rubbed everything in life,
a lonely woman, until her fingers
stopped asking questions. Now,
her body arches, spins—a golden
thumb and finger, grasping at stars,
rubbing the universe to keep it warm.

Downcast

Those who cast a bronze
know the lost wax must
go somewhere—a vapor
that gives way to form.
When the heat of creation
replaces me—when I give
way to some new shape
awaiting pairing and polish—
will anyone remember
that which was me for
all my years of sculpting?

Day Breaks

Day breaks
and we try
to fix it.

We fail
and night
falls.

Speech Therapy

People can say what they want
with words like windows
rattling in the wind
and what they say
is air articulated
through screens
and frames, fricatives,
sounds hanging like innuendos
stretching knotted necks,
shades like coatings on the tongue,
curtains of conspiracies
to silhouette the dead.

We break the glass, keyless,
open the windows wide
with promises of familiar
things but find the house
is empty, robbed
before we came.

People say "love"
like glass shattering,
but is there ever
anything to steal?

Child's Play

1.
A mother barks an order
at her three-year-old boy,
"Not another step." He
freezes and repeats,
"Not another step."
The bruises on the back
of his legs explain it.

2.
A seventh grader stops
showering after gym.
Too many drop-the-soap
jokes. He remembers
the rectal bleeding when
he was nine or ten.

3.
The little girl squirms on her
bicycle seat. It still hurts
where her uncle poked her.

4.
A young mother won't let her
daughter out of her sight.
It's been twenty years since
it happened to her but she'll
never let it happen to her kid.

Caged

A freight train complains its way through
the city, soft moans two miles away.
What do its cars contain that I really
need, lying here in my super-darkened
bedroom, a blanket protecting me?
My house is thirty degrees warmer
than the homeless who sleep secreted
among the dumpsters just miles away.
This is my cage. I've poured
a hundred thou into everything
from a granite kitchen to white
concrete drive—rapidly turning
orange from the sprinklers. I'm
surrounded by beach-casual furniture—
hardwood with rattan designs—
drawers stuffed with a lifetime
supply of undershirts; closets with
more clothes than I can ever wear.
The furnace fan clicks on, warm
breath of a beast roaming the house.
I pull the cover up as much to hide
as for comfort. Late winter, 5:40 a.m.
Why, just before civil dawn, as the sun
considers its return to a hard, flat beach,
do I lie awake as if waiting for some
keeper to bring me my morning meat?

The Climate Of Our Disposition

1.
The gray insignificance
of the interstate despite
the prating of a billboard
for an "Adult Superstore."

2.
The repetition of gas
stations and fast-food
chains sawing at farm-
land edging small towns.

3.
Sixteen wheelers with
hemorrhoidal drivers;
trailer-home retirees
traveling their last miles.

4.
Clear to overcast to
showers in less than
twenty miles. Sudden
sunshine with a rainbow.

Dark Thoughts

Dark thoughts are my best
friends. I welcome them
in bed, reassuring me that
those who want to hurt me
are just part of the show.
No, I'm not suicidal,
there's no need for mandatory
reporting—at least
no more than for those who
love Quentin Tarantino
or relish Grand Theft Auto.
For the interval before I
sleep, I drift through images
like whips whose marks are
subliminal not subdural.
Pain is not a memory, it's
an activity. You may say,
"pathology," but why?
Do people criticize climbers
for defying dying? Regularly,
I summon what frightens
me. I hold fear dear, script
it carefully—lowering
a final curtain into sleep.

Betrayal Is Better Served

Cold. I know you are thinking, "revenge,"
or perhaps you believe that a good twist
of a knife deep into the back produces
a searing pain. Not so. Those who betray
friendships break the trust like thin
ice breaking suddenly beneath one's feet.
Imagine the illusion of solidity, the silly
confidence that one can walk on water,
though the cold should be a hint not to
trust. Skate out, do a figure eight, smile
until the sudden crack and quicker fall
beneath the ice. That's betrayal for you.
Just when you think someone is good,
all that you know lets go. You're left
wondering if there are really air bubbles
trapped under the surface or if you'll die
of the brutal cold before you drown.

Dear Mary-Ann

(My friend who says my poems are so sad.)

Because I judge myself
I stand accused, tried,
condemned by my own
judge and jury. Because
I trap myself, I am caught,
caged, denied release by
me, the cagey trapper.
Because I choke myself
I gasp, utter strangled
cries, see my bulging
eyes in the mirror of
my strangler. Because
I need to love I feel
denied, ignored, unable
to love myself without
reprisals. Because I know
these things, I'm ignorant,
unable to appeal, go free,
breathe deeply, or feel
the warmth of love.
Because I say these
things, you say it's sad,
pitiable, unfortunate but
art is life made finer.
I find a pleasing symmetry
in this explanatory letter.

Politics In Four Beats

(Their dictators are imposed on them.
We elect ours. —Harry Kuhner)

1.
ISIS, the Taliban exploding ancient
ruins: savages, unconscionable,
except one third of Vienna destroyed
by Allied bombs; the ancient
landmarks of Budapest. Dresden.
Hiroshima justified by Pearl
Harbor, bombing London.

2.
800,000 homeless in the U.S.,
200,000 of them children.
A quarter of our children
live below poverty level.
No metaphors for hunger.

3.
The local daily, bought by arch
conservatives, has laid off most
beat reporters, buys syndicated news
and features supporting its point
of view. Front pages extend stories
about aging war heroes. Local

section—car crashes, drugs and
crime—little necessary news.

4.
Every four years it's Presidential
campaign time, debates, grand-
standing—negativity, lies
outright. Same game, different
day. Which haircut, which fool?
The head may change but
the body politic is moribund.

Even Diamonds Melt

At ground zero even
diamonds melt and burn.
At Hiroshima, a fraction
of a second, 6000+ degrees,
a supersonic shock wave,
intense radiation.
  10,000 people vaporized.
  40,000 more dead below the blast.
  90,000 killed nearby.
160,000 additional deaths.
300,000 total, but we round
such numbers avoiding actual
accountability. Does any
contender for major office
swear never to use
a nuclear bomb?

Late Train Out Of Manhattan

(September 11, 2001.)

They stopped taking tickets
when the LIRR resumed
late afternoon. Just ran
the trains out of NYC
for those who hadn't walked.
Earlier, the bridges swelled
with unaccustomed walkers —
a marathon of frightened men,
saddened women reminding
themselves to not look back
at columns of smoke, at what
was no longer there. By one a.m.
exhausted rescuers sitting
in stunned silence. At each station,
parking lots still too full of vehicles
waiting to confirm their owners lost.

Censorship

Each day I tear articles
from papers—today
a naked child, burned,
crying. Her photo,
it says, helped stop
the Vietnam war.
An army lieutenant
called in the strike
to flush out peasants
hiding in a temple.

Now they've found
the little girl, all grown,
and want to honor her.
She says that she
forgives them, though
their uniforms still
frighten her and she
still feels the pain
of them cutting
the dead skin.

I tear an article on
Wal-Mart, Kmart,
Blockbuster—how they
remove anything that
may offend their
customers—no dirty
words, no sacrilege,
no politics, sanitizing

album covers, lyrics,
softening their videos.

I fold these articles
to show my classes,
aware some blockhead,
conservative, anyone
empowered by the myth
he's right, could ask:
"What does this have
to do with English?"

I'm not teaching literature,
I'm teaching empathy.

Duty

It's not just the medals on your Marine
uniform, or your shaved head, or even spit-
polished shoes. It doesn't matter disciplinary
officers at your college don't understand
that swearing like a Marine in class is
not your problem. Screw them for not
understanding. Your father
was a Marine, your grandfather,
and you say you'd do your duty even
if you knew the orders were wrong.
Semper Fi! Do or Die! A sheepish grin,
confounding your professor's logic,
who asks you, "Why?" You went
to Iraq, he didn't. You saw a best friend
die, so who is he to ask you? Now,
they are paying for your education
and you want it, quickly, easily.
The hard part was getting here.
Why are these civilians trying
to teach you something?

Weapon Of Choice

I admire guns
their finality;
the vociferation
of a blade, too long;
the bludgeon's
argument diffuse.
A gun, point
not to be argued.

I admire the bullet,
proof that less is
more; not
the perturbation
of poison, nor
vagaries of accidents.
A bullet, end
of story.

But most, I admire
the target;
predestination
a question; the Gods
aloof; concentric
circles, truth.

Fifty Fifty

Moira, you whore, you sell yourself
to the rich. They can suffer in comfort.
Androgynous concubine, attacking
us from behind—the poor don't get
to chose their fate. The past we can
adjudicate. The future is fifty fifty.
We know the suchness of routine:
piecework, patchwork, low-paid
jobs; mindless work with no reward.
Dock workers, doctorates, taxi drivers,
derelicts, dilatants, all struck down
or rendered dumb by struggles to survive.
Dumb luck, first cousin to our fate,
equalizes us at last. Man tracht, und Got
lacht. The difference between deification
and defecation is in the i's of the beholder.
Just when you think you've won, along
comes Armageddon. Moira, you visited
yesterday, tied me to the bedposts, taunting,
"Try that again and you will die."
Mortality cures all—reducing us to epigrams,
recycled molecules, barely a blink in time.
Until then, we take our chances.

Foreseeing Change

The numbers runners are
always there to take our bets —
fortunes told with crystals,
cards; Kabbalist mysteries,
Daoists reading yarrow sticks.
Odds are they will tell us what
we want if we cross their palms
with silver. Fates rise and fall,
birds fly prophetically, or
is it all modern code — ones
and zeros that drive us?
Presidents, to this day, are
inaugurated. Who better to
lead us than an augur —
a prophet who will show
us the way? For all
the promises, the entrails
read, what is more
predictable than how
we are led to slaughter?

Morning Songs

Songs through your windows
are tires on rainy streets
already rushing to where
you need to be, like a desk
in an office where you poise
all day at a keyboard.
But there's your bed
and a fleeting thought
of calling the boss with
some song and dance
that you can't come in,
a euphemism for won't.
You sing in the shower,
let the towel whisper
to your skin. A damp
breeze from an open
window coaxes you
to leave. A glance back
at your pillow, still
impressed by your
sleepy head, and it's off
to the song of industry.

Acknowledgments

New poems: "Sun Worship," *South Florida Poetry Journal*; "Old Soul," *Long Island Quarterly* (Winter, 2015); "Seeing Things As They Are," "Shrinking," *Voices of Israel* (2015); "Not Fighting," *Long Island Quarterly* (Twenty-Fifth Anniversary, 2016); "Homeless in Daytona," *Cyclamens & Sword* (Fall, 2014); "Cockroach Immortality," "Whistling," *Cyclamens & Swords* (Winter, 2015); "Cop Story," *What It Means to Be White* (2Leaf Press, 2016); "Foreseeing Change," "Dear Mary-Ann," *Looking Life in the Eye: Poets of Central Florida* (Volume Three, 2015); "In Favor of a New Poet Laureate," *Florida Congressional Record* (April 23, 2014); "Seeing Things as They Are," *Thirty Three: An[niversary] Anthology* (Negative Capability, 2014); "Calling Out Their Names," *Protest Against Mass Incarceration* (Coalition for Justice, 2014); "The Recurring Metaphor," *Lone Star Magazine* (#82, 2016); "Caged," in a slightly different version, *Daytona News-Journal*; "From Such Mediations," *Yu Su Temple Newsletter*; "Disappearance," "The Savior," "On Being Safe," "Philosophical Differences," *Antarctica Journal*; "Day Breaks," *First Literary Review*; "The Climate of our Disposition," "Politics in Four Parts," *Suffolk County Poetry Journal*. "Calling Out Their Names," "Fifty Fifty," "Curing Rilke," "Fingering," "Celebrate Good Times," "Peg Leg Bates," "Surprises," *Laurels: Poetry from the Laureates of Long Island* (Local Gems Press, 2016). "Florida Haikus and Tankas" combines new and previous poems which have appeared in *Trapani Nuovo; A Perpetual Calendar of Poems* (C-CC Edition, Anti-Gruppo Siciliano, 1988) and *Rusting: Ways to Keep Living* (Taylor and Seale, 2014). "November," set to music as a libretto and performed by Matthew Pierce, and in *Perpetual Calendar*. Selected poems: "Clorox Clean," *Xanadu Magazine*; "The Snowbird's Sonnet," *The Hidden Zone*, and

A Calendar of Florida Poets (2013); "Bird Understanding," "The Buddhist Bird," *DaoUSA Newsletter*, also included in *Rusting*. "Autographs," *Valparaiso Poetry Review*; "Thanks to Doppler," both in *The SPEED Way* (TotalRecall Publications, 2012, 2nd Edition, 2014). "Beach Countdown," *Deciduous* (Ahadada Books, 2008). Poems from the book, *Deciduous*, also appeared in the following: "Little League," *Conceit Magazine*; "The Last Time My Father Beat Me," first prize, *Rogue Scholars*; "Duty," *The Improper Hamptonian*; "For His Son," *Oberon* poetry award, and *Teleisian*; "It's a Happy Man," *Poetrybay*; "For the Valentine I Don't Have," *Long Island Eagle*; "Morning Songs," *Enskyment*; "Late Train Out of Manhattan," *The Light of City and Sea* (North Sea Poetry Press, 2008), and *Duke's Broadside Series* (2001). "Parenting," *Another Way: Poems Derived from the Tao Te Ching* (Karma Dog, 2005; 2nd Edition, Mighty Rogue Press, 2014). "Weapon of Choice," *Eat-Write Café, Pedestal,* and in *The Impossibility of Dreams* (Ahadada Books, 2007). "On Reading *A Brief History of Time,*" "Soccer," "The Full Moon," "Robert Frost," "The Lifetime Channel," "Random Beauty," "Censorship," *Random Beauty* (Amereon House, 2001). Poems in *Random Beauty* also appeared in the following: "A Guide to Suburban Birds," *Urban Nature* (Milkweed Press, 2000); "Seder in a Jewish Nursing Home," *Jewish Dialog*. Poems in *Love in the Keys* (Ai Press, 1991, 2001) also appeared in the following: "The Slaughter," *Long Island Quarterly*, and *Shikhan* (Guangzhou); "Eating Their Hearts Out," "Watching You," "Kissing in Front of the Microwave," *Passaic Review*; "Kissing in Front of the Microwave," *LIPS*. "Eating Their Hearts Out," *A Taste of Poetry* (Walt Whitman Birthplace Association, 2015). "On Reading *A Brief History of Time,*" *The Chi of Poetry* (Published with a grant while on Fulbright by American/ People's Press, Birnham Wood Graphics, 1995). Poems in *Chi* also appeared in the following: "Heroics," *Long Island Quarterly*, and *Literary Works* (Guangzhou); "The Pro," "Spring the Age-Old Question," *Poets and Artists Interpreting the Island* (The Museums at Stony Brook, 1991). Thanks to the Fulbright Commission for publication of the bilingual Macedonian/English book, *Resurrections*

(C-CC Edition, Nasha Kniga: Skopia, Macedonia, 1989), distributed in Yugoslavia for Dr. Axelrod's term as Poet-in-Residence and Fulbright professor at Skopia University. "Poems in *Resurrections* also appeared in the following: "For Gail, Who Called Herself Charlie," *Lilith*; "Pickling," *Xanadu*; "Seeing the Specialist," in Serbo-Croatian, *Journal of Struga International Poetry Evenings*, and *Confrontation*; "The Critical Weakness," *West Hills Review*. "Midwinter, Stony Brook Harbor" was read as the Inaugural Poem for Suffolk County Executive, Steve Levy, by Dr. Axelrod as Suffolk County Poet Laureate. Many poems also appeared in translation in Italian, on the arts "Page Three" of *Trapani Nuovo* (Sicily), and in the following magazines: *Bluefish; Pearl; Long Pond Review; Island Light: Suffolk Bi-Centennial Anthology*. "White Lies," "Pile On," "Faith," *White Lies* (La Jolla Poets Press, 1988). "A Lesson in Friendship," "The End of the Universe," *The Greenfield Review*, and *The End of the Universe* (CRI Productions, 1987). Poems from the book, *Home Remedies* (Cross-Cultural Communications, 1982) also appeared in the following: "The Suffering Goes Both Ways," *Blood to Remember: American Poets on the Holocaust* (Time Being Books, 2005) "Elegies for My Family," "We Are All Hit and Run," *Trapani Nuovo* (bilingually, Sicily, Italy); "Nanny and Zayde," *PLA Report* (C.W. Post Library Association); "Two Sonnets in Fear of Cancer," *Crop Dust*, and *Trapani Nuovo*; "Campsite Eraclea-Minoa, Sicily," painted by Arnold Hoffman, Jr., for *Artists and Poets of the Hamptons* (Guild Hall, 1982), and *Trapani Nuovo, Zephyr*; "One for My Father," *Confrontation*, and *Bluefish*; "Weather Patterns," "The Vandal," "Curiosity," "Campsite Eraclea-Minoa," also appeared in *Zephyr*; "The Vandal" was winner of Academy of American Poets, C.W. Post Award presented by Richard Wilbur. "The Man Who Fell in Love With His Chicken," "Tongue Hotel," *New Letters*, and *The Man Who Fell in Love With a Chicken* (Cross-Cultural Communications, 1980). "Smell My Fingers," first appeared in *A Dream of Feet* (Cross-Cultural Communications, 1975). Poems from *Feet* also appeared in the following: "Once in a While a Protest Poem," *The Voyeur*, then and in four editions of X. J. Kennedy's

Introduction to Literature and *Introduction to Poetry*; "The Dead Have No Respect," *Literature: Introduction to Fiction, Poetry and Drama* (X. J. Kennedy, Dana Gioia, editors. Editions 7 & 8, Longman, 1999); "Contact Myth," *Carolina Quarterly*; "A Short Course on the Holocaust," *Town of Islip Poetry Festival Pamphlet* (1973). "We Need What We Want," "½ Scientist, ½ Woman," *Myths, Dreams and Dances* (Despa Press, 1974). Poems in *Myths* also appeared in the following: "Mother and Child," *New York University School of Medicine Literature and Medicine Data Base* (http://medhum.med.nyu.edu/person/2348); "He Was Calm," *The Freelance*; "Gimme Culture," *Measured Mile*; "Alone in Your House," *Kansas Quarterly*, *Vagabond* and *The Best of Vagabond Anthology* (1973). "Old Age Can Be Heroic," *Pressluft* (Austria), *Trapani Nuovo* (Sicily), *Novi Macedonski* (Skopia, Macedonia), *Starting from Paumanok* (Despa Press, 1971). "Widows," "Girl at a Sidewalk Café," *Stills from a Cinema* (Despa Press, 1968, 1971).